Dear Chris and Halley,

 I'm so fortunate to have you as friends. I hope you enjoy these recipes and take the opportunity to visit some of these fabulous inns.

Love,
Debby

2-19-

A scenic tour of Pacific Northwest inns with selected recipes

A Taste for Comfort

Anita Stewart

C&D Publishing
Portland, Oregon

A Taste For Comfort
A scenic tour of Pacific Northwest inns with selected recipes
Author: Anita Stewart

Library of Congress Catalog Card Number 92-76126
ISBN 0-9634294-0-X

Manufactured in the United States of America

C&D Publishing,
1017 SW Morrison #500
Portland, Oregon 97205
(503) 274–8780

Project coordination: Sharon Van Loan
Inns coordination: Rosanne Allenby
Book design: Kim Roadruck Graphic Design, Portland, Oregon
Typesetting: Admiral Typesetting, Portland, Oregon
Print brokerage: Robert Dierkes, A Graphic Resource, St. Louis, Missouri

Contents

Washington

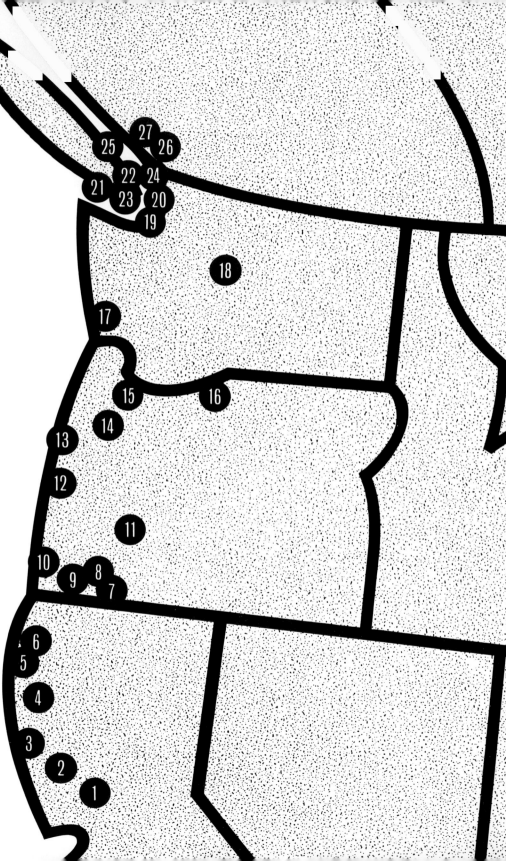

"Tis the reader that makes the good book." —Emerson
For the late M.F.K. Fisher

This book was written for the serious traveler, the person who loves to explore, the adventurer who can hardly wait to see what lies around the next bend. It is also written for the serious gourmet who loves great regional food and subscribes to the wise philosophy that only by eating local foods can one dine on the very best.

The members of The Unique Northwest Country Inns share that belief in the value of regional produce. Without exception they buy from local growers, searching out new, and sometimes ancient, ingredients. Some of them have fostered the growth of a whole new set of producers. They frequent farm markets. They are innovative—one scubas for his shellfish. They are famous—most of them have been acknowledged by leading food writers and have been featured in publications the world over. But in other ways these inns are not alike. As the name of the association implies, each is unique.

In visiting these inns I have expanded old horizons and come to admire this vast, wild stretch of the Pacific Northwest—from the Redwoods of California to the mountains and islands of British Columbia. I love its great wines and the innkeepers themselves; I have gained 50 new friends. The same will happen to you in your travels. You will eat new dishes, play new games, travel new highways and even a few dusty country roads. You will visit tiny wineries, talk to local folks and fall in love, if you haven't already, with this superb part of the world.

—Anita Stewart

Special thanks to Erin Caldwell of B.C. Ferries, Coval Air from Campbell River, Helijet Airways, Joyce Brookbank of Tourism Vancouver Island, Jamie Douglas of Sonoma County Visitors Bureau and Donna Depauli of Eureka/Humboldt County Visitors and Convention Bureau. I also greatly appreciate the assistance of Rosanne Allenby and Sharon Van Loan—their sharp attention to detail, their follow through and many hours of work on this project helped tremendously.

Wine Country Inn
Madrona Manor
Harbor House—Inn by the Sea

Benbow Inn
The Gingerbread Mansion
The Carter House/Hotel Carter

Northern California

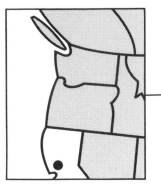

The Wine Country Inn

Late at night, driving along Highway 29, it became apparent that we were on the Royal Road of Wineries. Opus I, Mondavi, Beaulieu, all fabulously lit, lay nestled in the darkness. Few valleys on earth could appeal so to the senses. Frogs' contralto choruses echoed across the valley, green in spring, now multi-colored with red and green fruit accented against a golden autumn background. The smells from the warm soil surrounded us as we drove along, enjoying the raucous songs of flock after flock of sparrows.

The Wine Country Inn could hardly have a better location. It is down the road or, in some cases, just next door to some of Napa's best wineries. It was founded by Jim Smith's parents and four siblings. While older brother Doug was the foreman, Jim took over the stonemasonry. "Dad didn't want it to be another Victorian, he wanted it to look indigenous," says Jim. Gardens were planted—"It's a real challenge to keep them under control"—and an inground pool and spa were added at the base of a steep terrace. Long purple wisteria drape over a latticework arbor. Rosemary bushes grow tall, covered with their spicy-scented blue flowers.

The inn's balconies are protected by olive trees that, when I was there, were totally loaded with ripe fruit. Jim has promised that very soon he will start to cure the olives. From these private porticos, particularly those in the Brandy Barn, guests can watch the morning mists flow over the vineyards. The room I stayed in was rustic and woodsy, reminiscent of the Southwest. Jim's mother, who now lives just up the lane, sewed the quilts; his

grandmother did the stitcheries for the walls and his sister Kate, a country and western singer, made the hangings. Terra cotta lamps lighted my room, reflecting on the high oaken bedstead.

The Wine Country Inn offers a light breakfast to its guests...lots of fruit, granola and quick breads...and of course, after all the wine-tasting the day before, there's good, strong coffee.

Say "Napa Valley" and immediately great wine comes to mind. "Ninety percent of our guests come to do the wine tour," says Jim. Thirty miles long, the

valley lies between two ridges, the Mayacamas range in the west and the Vaca hills to the east. Its climate is definitely Mediterranean. The first vineyard was planted by George Yount in 1838. Charles Krug followed in 1858. From 1890 until Prohibition, the land planted to grapes remained at roughly 10,000 acres. Prohibition set the industry back almost to square one. Only a handful of vineyards survived, among them Krug, Beringer and Inglenook.

The revival began in the 1960s when the cabernet, merlot and chardonnay vines were planted. But it wasn't until 1976, when Chateau Montelena

Chardonnay and Stag's Leap Wine Cellars' Cabernet Sauvignon placed first in a Parisian wine competition organized by Stephen Spurrier, that Californian wines became a force with which to be reckoned and enjoyed.

A more recent major development in the valley has been the professional marriage of wine with food. Robert Mondavi launched his Great Chefs program and recently Beringer has opened its Culinary Arts Center. The Culinary Institute of America, based in Hyde Park, New York, is developing a branch in the 100-year-old building, formerly the Christian Brothers Winery.

You can walk to some wineries from The Wine Country Inn, a particularly nice feature if you plan on tasting more than the usual quota. Duckhorn is just down Lodi Lane. It's a lovely stroll beside a row of live oak trees and over a stone fence to Folie a Deux or down a newly cleared path to Freemark Abbey.

One of the best ways to get your bearings and a great way to begin a Napa visit is to do the Gourmet Tour by taxi with Cabernet Tours. Owner David Mitchell knows the valley intimately and takes visitors either to the big names like Inglenook and Charles Krug or to his own favorites among smaller, less famous wineries. If you choose to do a self-guided tour, The Wine Country Inn staff can recommend half a dozen favorites. Jim feels that his task as innkeeper is to narrow the choice from 260 or so wineries to a manageable number. In particular, Robert Mondavi should not be missed.

If you are a history buff, you will surely enjoy Beringer's. It is a significant historical landmark and the tour guides will fill you in with stories and anecdotes. Another memorable experience is a ride on a tram up to the winery that doubles as a castle, Sterling Vineyards. Grigich Cellars features Mike

Grigich who made the chardonnay for Chateau Montelena that won in Paris in 1976. He continues every year to produce award-winning varietals. At Joseph Phelps Winery you will have one of the best tours in Napa. Finally, be sure not to miss Chateau Montelena itself, a fairy castle, just north of Calistoga.

The Wine Country Inn

1152 Lodi Lane
St. Helena, California 94574
(707) 963–7077/(800) 473–3463
FAX: (707) 963–9018
Innkeeper: Jim Smith

Wine Country Inn Granola

This is their most called-for recipe.

> *2 c old-fashioned rolled oats*
> *1 c slivered or sliced almonds*
> *¼ c melted butter*
> *¼ c honey*
> *¼ c brown sugar*
> *sprinkle of cinnamon and salt*
> *1 c flaked coconut*
> *1 c raisins*

Preheat oven to 325°F.

In a large lightly oiled baking pan, mix together oats and almonds. In a small bowl, stir together the butter and honey; pour over oats, mixing well. Sprinkle with brown sugar, cinnamon and salt, stirring thoroughly.

Bake until light brown, stirring frequently. Mix in coconut; continue to bake until medium brown. Remove from oven; add raisins. Stir frequently while cooling. Store in tightly covered container.

MAKES EIGHT TO TEN SERVINGS.

Whole Wheat Banana Bread

Whole wheat flour enriches the flavor of this moist banana bread. It has a wonderful, light, cake-like texture.

½ c butter or margarine, melted
1 c granulated sugar
2 eggs, slightly beaten
1 c ripe bananas, about 3 medium, mashed
½ tsp salt
1 tsp baking soda
1 c all purpose flour, measured before sifting
1 c whole wheat flour
⅓ c hot water
½ c chopped walnuts

Beat together melted butter and sugar. Whip in eggs, one at a time. Add bananas, blending until smooth. Sift salt, soda and all purpose flour together; combine with whole wheat flour.

Add dry ingredients to creamed mixture alternately with hot water. Stir in chopped nuts. Turn into well-greased 9 x 5 inch baking pan.

Preheat oven to 325°F. Bake for one hour and 10 minutes or until a skewer inserted into loaf comes out clean.

Let cool on wire rack. Store in air-tight container.

Makes one loaf.

Jim's Two Day Tacos

This dish was named "two day" because it takes one day to prepare and one day to clean up the mess! To serve, fill hot taco shells with meat, shredded lettuce, diced tomatoes, sour cream, salsa and shredded cheese.

2 ½ lb beef chuck roast
flour as needed to dredge meat
¼ c vegetable oil
2 onions, coarsely chopped
5 large cloves garlic, minced
3 bottles dark beer
3 bell peppers, coarsely chopped
3 Anaheim peppers, coarsely chopped
2 Tbl California chili powder (mild)
2 Tbl cumin
salt to taste
1 can (16 oz) stewed tomatoes (optional)

Flour meat well. Heat oil in large, heavy saucepot. Brown meat thoroughly on all sides. Remove and set aside.

Add onions to hot oil, browning deeply. Remove and set aside. Drain any excess fat. Add garlic, cooking for 15 to 20 seconds. Add half a bottle of beer to pan, stirring to loosen browned bits.

Return meat and onions to pan; cover with beer. Simmer, uncovered, for two hours, adding beer as needed to keep meat covered. Stir to keep from sticking. Add peppers; continue to cook for one hour.

With slotted spoon, remove meat from broth.

When meat is cool enough to handle, cut away gristle and shred. Add to broth with any remaining beer. Stir in chili powder, cumin and tomatoes.

Continue to cook until broth is reduced to almost nothing. Stir often to prevent burning.

Makes six to eight servings.

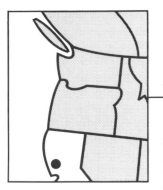

Madrona Manor

Sonoma County, California. "I firmly believe, from what I have seen, that this is the chosen spot of all this earth as far as Nature is concerned."—Luther Burbank, on his arrival in Santa Rosa in 1875.

Other famous Americans have chosen Sonoma County, the lush region north of San Francisco, above all others. Days are filled with sun and flowers; the nights smell of the warmed earth, and boisterous choruses of frogs take over from the daytime cicadas.

In the springtime, it pulses with the promise of life. The dormant vineyards are streaked with the wild yellow of mustard flowers. Ripening summer seems hot and languorous for months on end. It is the land of Jack London and his beloved Valley of the Moon.

The county borders the Pacific Ocean with its salmon fishery and oyster beds. Over 130 wineries populate Sonoma's 11 viticultural areas covering 32,000 acres of vineyards. It's a bit like a who's who of the winemaking industry from the opulent Jordan Winery, with its French chateau architecture, to the homespun Martinelli vineyards clinging to the steep banks of Jackass Hill.

The people of this sun-splashed county have one characteristic in common: They are acutely aware of their natural blessings. And few are louder boosters of "Sonoma Grown" than the Muir family of Madrona Manor. You will regularly see John Muir trekking down to the local farmers' market as much to pick up the freshest produce as to chat with his grower friends. Back in the kitchen, son Todd, a supremely

talented chef, is "writing the book" on the new Sonoma cuisine.

Madrona Manor is a place of hidden treasures and refined elegance. On a spring day sunlight spills over the hills and through the eight-foot French doors. It's almost impossible to stay in bed on such tantalizing California days.

In 1881 wealthy businessman John Paxton began construction of Madrona Knoll Rancho. With its 17 rooms, seven fireplaces and three full baths, it was a source of great pride for the community of Healdsburg. When the Muirs purchased it, the gates had been padlocked for 17 years, entwined with trees that had 12 and 15 inch trunks. It was in desperate need of repair. I'm not sure who deserves more credit, John Paxton or the industrious Muir family who dealt with its peculiarities and years of neglect.

The interior is filled, as it should be, with mahogany and rosewood. A square grand piano that dates from the last half of the 19th century is still tuned well enough that after a couple of glasses of wine, it doesn't matter. Outdoors, the gardens are thick with flowers and fruit trees. Innkeeper Carol Muir makes gallons of marmalade from the dwarf mandarin orange trees. If you love gardening, bring a camera. Madrona Manor is a showplace.

If you have time to explore, one of the best guides is a Sonoma County Farm Trails map; mine literally fell apart with use. It'll coax you onto the region's backroads. You will meet delightful producers like Bonnie and Malcolm Yuill-Thornton at Dragonfly Farm just down the road from Madrona Manor. On their six acre plot they grow over 200 varieties of

plants, such as the locally hybridized Crane melons and the sweetest cherry tomatoes you'll ever taste. Search out Yak-a-ama, a native teaching center, near Forestville, which focuses on the preservation and understanding of native plant material. There is even a small gift shop devoted to hand-crafted items from the local Ohlone community.

Try to schedule a trip in concert with the Sonoma Country Farmlands Wine and Food Series. They are held at intervals throughout the summer at a variety of county wineries. For a small fee you can taste and sip the wares of 20 or 30 of the best new and often rare vintages and food samples ranging

from Brother Juniper's filled stromboli breads to Clover-Stornetta's delicious local cheeses.

Madrona Manor

1001 Westside Road,
Box 818
Healdsburg, California 95448
(707) 433–4231/(800) 258–4003
FAX: (707) 433–0703
Innkeepers: John and Carol Muir

Range Veal on Rosemary Brochettes with Blueberry Sauce

Serve this pungently seasoned meat with wild rice and a wonderful huge salad packed with as many exotic greens as you can find.

> 2 lb range veal leg, cleaned of fat and silver skin
> 12 rosemary branches, about 4–5 inches long
> 1 Tbl chopped rosemary leaves
> ½ cup olive oil
> ½ cup dry white wine
> 1 ½ tsp freshly cracked pepper

Cut meat into one inch cubes. Remove lower leaves from rosemary branches, leaving on top leaves. Skewer three cubes veal on each branch. Place in a 9 x 13 inch glass baking pan. Combine chopped rosemary, olive oil, white wine and cracked pepper. Pour over meat; cover and refrigerate for at least two hours. Grill over mesquite charcoal turning for 10 minutes or until done. Allow two skewers per person. Moisten with Blueberry Sauce.

Blueberry Sauce

About 30 minutes before grilling the veal, whip up the following sauce.

> 1 c whole blueberries
> ¼ cup granulated sugar
> 1 tin (10 oz) low salt beef broth
> 2 c blueberry wine
> juice of 1 lemon or to taste

Purée half of the blueberries; set aside. Reserve remaining whole berries.

In a heavy saucepan, heat sugar over medium heat until it begins to melt and turn golden brown. Stir constantly until it is dark. Immediately pour in broth, wine and blueberry *purée*. Bring to a boil over medium high heat; cook, uncovered, until volume is reduced to about one cup. Stir in remaining whole berries and lemon juice to taste.

MAKES ENOUGH SAUCE FOR SIX SERVINGS.

Goat Cheese Wonton Soup

California is famous for its goat cheese, showcased here in a light, elegant clear soup.

Wontons

> 3 oz goat cheese, crumbled
> 1 Tbl minced chives
> salt and freshly ground pepper to taste
> 1 egg white
> ¼ c water
> 12 wonton skins

Soup

> 2 Tbl diced cooked egg white
> 2 Tbl thinly sliced fresh shiitake
> 1 Tbl thinly sliced green onion
> 8 paper-thin slices garlic
> 8 paper-thin slices ginger
> 8 fine strands orange zest
> 4 c rich clear chicken stock, heated

Garnish

> 8 cilantro leaves
> hot chili oil to taste

To make the wontons, combine goat cheese, chives, salt and pepper to taste. Whisk egg white with water to make egg wash.

Place 1 ½ teaspoons goat cheese mixture on center of each wonton wrapper. Brush edges with egg wash; fold to create triangle; pinch closed. Fold the opposite corners of triangle around finger, moisten with egg wash and press firmly together.

Poach wontons in a pot of simmering salted water for three minutes. Remove with slotted spoon. Divide among four heated soup bowls. To each bowl, add egg white, mushrooms, green onion, garlic, ginger and orange zest. Add hot chicken stock; garnish with cilantro leaves and a few drops of hot chili oil.

MAKES FOUR SERVINGS.

20

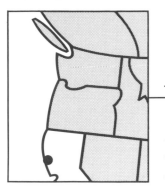

Harbor House–Inn by the Sea

Harbor House is one of the most comfortable inns in the entire Northwest. Dean and Helen Turner make the art of hospitality look incredibly easy and feel incredibly good. Their style is casual, their inn is warm, their food is honest and tastes of its rural heritage.

We drove the fabled Highway 1 in a soaking rain, a welcome downpour to this too long parched coastline. Mendocino lay to the north, all cute little California galleries and emporiums. The fog began to sweep inland making the curving road a challenge even for a well-tuned Mercedes.

Arriving at the precise, pitch dark dot of 7:00pm, the pre-ordained hour when dinner is served, we dashed inside to be greeted by a dancing fire and a bottle of garnet Caymus Vineyards zinfandel. A light carrot soup had a powerful mint leaf garnish, great with the just-baked lemon thyme bread. Often there is an exceptional sourdough bread, made by a purist baker who goes so far as to actually collect wild yeasts. A sage and garlic marinated pork loin had been grilled over mesquite by a chef holding an umbrella. Thin slices were served with a tart wild huckleberry sauce. The vegetables were local and very fresh. A warm bowlful of apple crisp, made with apples gathered at nearby Greenwood and served with inn-made caramel ice cream, was the finale.

The surf awoke me, resounding from the black hulking rocks that slowly appeared from the night. On the horizon a sliver of moonlight still glowed. In bed, I watched the day begin. It was an unequalled welcome to the wild Mendocino coastline.

Ernest Braun

By the time I broke my reverie, the smell of coffee was already in the hall. The fire had been started in the redwood panelled living area's fireplace. In that golden, high-ceilinged room, it is easy to understand why Harbor House is architecturally significant. Built in 1916 from virgin redwood from the nearby Albion forest, it is an enlarged version of the Home of the Redwood building from the 1915 Panama-Pacific International Exposition in San Francisco, designed by Louis Christian Mullgardt.

Outside, king rooster was sporadically crowing on top of the chicken coop while overseeing "the girls," a flock of multi-colored hens that seem happy to lay all the eggs the inn's cooks can want.

Helen and Dean have created two sorts of gardens, one full of vegetables, herbs and salad greens, all neatly laid out in raised beds; the other wild and tangled, full of berries and calla lilies and plate-sized nasturtium leaves spilling down the cliff. The inn is surrounded by mature trees including a huge cypress. Helen uses the cedar as a base for her cellar-made potpourri which she leaves for every guest.

The nicest room in the inn is also the smallest. They have named it "The Lookout," and its delicate white iron bedstead and huge rippled glass windows make stay-a-beds feel as if they are floating above the surf. Its deck is a personal perch overlooking the ocean.

Harbor House–Inn by the Sea

5600 S. Highway 1
Box 369
Elk, California 95432
(707) 877–3203
Innkeepers: Helen and Dean Turner

Minted Pea Soup

The Elk/Greenwood area is known for its peas. Here, Helen pays homage to them. Serve the soup piping hot or chilled.

> *3 leeks, cleaned and finely chopped*
> *1 medium onion, minced*
> *2 Tbl butter*
> *5 c good quality chicken stock*
> *2 handfuls fresh mint leaves*
> *2 c freshly shelled peas, or*
> *2 c tiny frozen peas (more for thicker soup)*
> *salt and freshly ground pepper to taste*
> *1 cup light cream (10%) (optional)*
> *yogurt or sour cream, fresh mint leaves for garnish*

In a heavy saucepan, *sauté* the leeks and onions in the butter until tender, about five or six minutes.

Stir in stock; bring to a boil. Chop mint coarsely; add to broth with peas. If using frozen peas, take off heat and let cool. If using fresh, reduce heat and simmer two to five minutes, depending on age of peas, until tender.

Purée soup in blender or food processor; return to clean pan. Reheat, seasoning with salt and pepper to taste. Stir in cream. Garnish with a spoonful of yogurt or sour cream; top with mint sprig.

MAKES SIX TO EIGHT SERVINGS.

Spinach Salad with Feta and Almonds

Of all their excellent salads, this is my favourite.

Herb Vinaigrette

> *¼ c balsamic vinegar*
> *1 Tbl soy sauce*
> *1 Tbl honey*
> *1 clove garlic, crushed*
> *1 Tbl chopped, fresh tarragon*
> *1 tsp dry mustard*
> *½ tsp paprika*
> *freshly ground pepper to taste*
> *½ c olive oil*

Salad

> *6 c spinach greens*
> *½ lb feta cheese, crumbled*
> *1 c toasted sliced almonds*

In a glass bowl or jar, blend the vinegar, soy, honey, garlic, tarragon, mustard, paprika, pepper and olive oil. Let stand for at least an hour before using.

Toss spinach with enough dressing to lightly coat leaves. Arrange on salad plates. Sprinkle with crumbled feta and almonds.

MAKES FOUR SERVINGS.

Gingered Greenwood Apple Crisp

> *10 large tart apples, peeled, cored and thinly sliced*
> *2 Tbl lemon juice*
> *1 ¼ c unbleached all purpose flour*
> *¾ c granulated sugar*
> *¾ c brown sugar, lightly packed*
> *2 oz crystallized ginger, finely chopped*
> *¾ c butter, chilled, cut into small pieces*

Preheat oven to 375°F. Toss apples with lemon juice. Arrange them in a shallow two and one-half quart ovenproof glass baking dish. Press down lightly to create a smooth surface.

With electric mixer or by hand, thoroughly combine flour, sugars and chopped ginger. Cut in butter until consistency of coarse meal. Sprinkle evenly over apples.

Bake for 40 minutes or until slightly browned. Serve warm or at room temperature with caramel ice cream.

MAKES TEN TO TWELVE SERVINGS.

Caramel Ice Cream

Believe me, for a caramel lover, it's really worth the fuss! The chef cautions that the caramel base should not be allowed to become too dark or the end result will be bitter. If it is too light, the ice cream will be excessively sweet.

> 1 c granulated sugar
> ¾ c water
> 2 c whipping cream, scalded
> 1 ½ c milk
> 8 large egg yolks

Combine sugar and water in medium sized, heavy saucepan that does not have a dark interior. Heat over low heat until sugar is dissolved. Increase heat to medium and boil without stirring until mixture is rich brown. A pastry brush dipped in water may be used occasionally to brush down crystals from side of pan. When richly golden, remove from heat. Carefully whisk in scalded cream. Cool, stirring constantly, until mixture stops bubbling. Whisk in milk. Return to medium-low heat; bring to simmer.

Lightly whisk egg yolks in large bowl. Gradually whisk in caramel mixture. Return to medium-low heat, stirring and scraping the bottom of pan until mixture thickens slightly. It will take five to seven minutes. Do not overcook, but cook completely.

Transfer to ice cream maker and freeze according to manufacturer's instructions. Scrape into chilled bowl or storage container; cover tightly and store in freezer until ready to serve. Let soften at room temperature before scooping.

MAKES ONE QUART.

Gramp's Oatmeal Bread

Claudia is one of Harbor House's longtime bakers. This is her grandfather's recipe.

> 1 c old-fashioned rolled oats
> 1 ½ c boiling water
> ½ c warm water
> 1 tsp granulated sugar
> 2 Tbl active dry yeast
> ⅓ c vegetable oil or melted butter
> ⅓ c molasses
> 1 ½ tsp salt
> 2 eggs
> 5–6 c all purpose flour, part whole wheat if desired

Place oatmeal into medium bowl, cover with boiling water. Let stand until lukewarm. In separate bowl, stir together warm water and sugar; sprinkle with yeast. Let stand 10 minutes or until puffed.

Mix cooled oat mixture with yeast mixture, oil, molasses, salt and beaten eggs. Stir in flour, a cupful at a time, until stiff enough to knead. Turn out onto floured surface, knead until smooth and elastic, about five to seven minutes. Place in lightly oiled bowl, cover with damp towel and let rise until doubled in bulk, about one and one-half hours. Punch down, divide into two loaves and place in well-greased 9 x 5 inch loaf pans. Let rise a second time until doubled.

Preheat oven to 400°F. Bake for 10 minutes; reduce heat to 350°F and finish baking for 20 minutes.

MAKES TWO LOAVES.

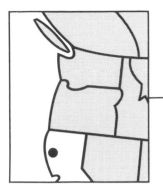

Benbow Inn

Once again the Benbow Inn is in its glory. With meticulous attention to small detail, Chuck and Patsy Watts have rebuilt the vintage hotel to an opulence the Benbow family would love. And, like all great innkeepers, they have injected a healthy dose of their own personalities. It's a place of teddy bears and roses, of great wines and vintage movies.

In the lobby, an eclectic mix of part of Chuck's clock collection, delicate needlepoint, wooden statuary and sumptuously upholstered couches surround chess players who are waging a fierce match. In the corner, a couple tests their skill at puzzle building. Meanwhile guests, pinkies in the air, sip tea from china cups and daintily spoon jam onto their cream scones. Theirs is not an unjustifiable hunger. After a swim in the soft river water of Lake Benbow or a bike ride down the quiet Northern California roads, lined with old madrone trees, it is quite understandable.

In 1922, the Benbow family purchased 1,288 acres of land at the confluence of the East Branch and the South Fork of the Eel River. Amidst the redwood groves and ruddy-trunked madrone trees, they had decided to become ranchers. It did not seem to work out too well, so they turned their thoughts to building a wonderful hotel. Starry-eyed optimists, they thought that the world would travel hundreds of miles, down twisting dusty highways to stay with them. After all, it took only 14 hours to get from San Francisco. Could Los Angelinos and New Yorkers be far behind?

Family members surveyed San Francisco and

Faith Echtermeyer

25

Oakland; when they saw a home that struck their fancy, they boldly made a visit to ask the architect's name. "Albert Farr" was the response so many times that they contracted him to begin the drawings. The lovely Hotel Benbow was underway. A modified English Tudor style, many of the mouldings were made by Burt Benbow in a little mill he erected on the site. Not only did he do the actual milling, he had to make the metal knives that were used to create the intricate designs. Overcoming a telephone company that closed the lines at 9:00pm and the lack of a building supply merchant, the doors were opened to the public in 1928. The Depression and World War II put a halt to additional construction, and when the Wattses took it over in 1978, they completed what the Benbow family had begun five decades earlier.

During the early years, a nine-hole golf course was scraped out of the hilly terrain by a team of mules. It's still a favorite among golfing guests, but as Patsy says, "You have to hit it straight down the line, or you'll be in the brambles."

The Benbows were not hoteliers, so some of their innovations didn't work too well. A huge water supply was needed for both the kitchen and for guests. Two used wine tanks were dutifully set into place above the hotel. The water tasted, and probably smelled, of old wine. They were quickly replaced.

When the arched stone bridge was built on old Highway 101, talk turned to a dam. It was to provide electricity and a swimming hole. Tenders were let, but the bids that came in caused the local officials to back out. After considerable deliberation, the Benbows decided to build the dam themselves. They had the good common sense of most rural folk and were not afraid of work. In 1931, the dam and fish ladder were

27

Bob Von Norman

completed under the watchful eyes of local skeptics who placed bets on when it would cave in. The power supplied the inn, and the lake thus formed has provided water recreation ever since. Today summer life still revolves around 26-acre Benbow Lake. In the 1950s, the state assumed responsibility for its protection, and today the park boasts 1,200 acres. Around Memorial Day, park officials drop boards into the cofferdam, and the lake fills. Area children learn to swim in the 10 to 12-foot depths. Boaters canoe the quiet waters. There's even the odd sailboard.

The inn overlooks the activity from a vantage point on the flower-covered hill. Protected from the winter winds by a high hedge, Patsy's rose garden is magnificent. At night, it perfumes the entire area. Hanging baskets droop from moss-covered trees, and in spring rhododendrons splash the property with color. The herb garden is in a sunny spot at the front of the inn. Lemon thyme blooms carpet-like under the red-flowered pineapple sage. Scented geraniums ring a buckeye tree. Beside the driveway is a row of chestnuts which will find their way into soups and the fruit stuffing for the Christmas goose. The gnarled old greening apple tree yields a couple of cases a year. In the backyard, under the live oaks and amongst more herbs, the inn has its own smokehouse.

These prolific gardens spice up the dishes which tempt guests all day long. Breakfast is a big event in the rosewood-adorned dining room. It can be as light as a platter of juicy California fruit with a dollop of yogurt or as substantial as a comforting bowl of oatmeal with apple, raisins, walnuts and a dusting of cinnamon. How could anyone resist the orange hazelnut waffle? It's the sort of dish that you see coming to another table and immediately regret not ordering.

The dining room fills quickly for dinner with guests ready to savour every mouthful. A whole onion is made into a surrealistic flower and baked with a few strips of proscuitto. Before serving, it is dusted with Parmesan cheese and drizzled with an herb vinaigrette. It was one of the most delicious warm salads I have had. A chilled red cabbage salad is blessed with a balsamic dressing before being sprinkled with walnuts and pungent Roquefort cheese. The cream of tomato soup is well seasoned with roasted garlic. The menu reflects the use of the best and freshest ingredients, rather than a multiplicity of items. If you choose the halibut, know that it will be snowy white and perfectly cooked. Vegetables are tender crisp. A hearty serving of pasta is regularly topped with exotic mushrooms and wonderful vegetables. But save a bit of room for dessert, perhaps a small slice. Try the white chocolate poppyseed torte with fresh berries, their fabulous chocolate mousse pie—or whatever else the pastry chef has concocted!

Master Benson Bear, Patsy's dear friend, loves a party, especially a tea party held in his honor each May. It began as a whim, and now everyone brings their teddys. Well-washed bears play croquet and later gather for a social time. Heart scones are served with Pooh honey and lemon curd and jams galore. Naturally there are watercress sandwiches and Paddington's tea cake. Hot cocoa with whipped cream is provided for persnickety bears, but for the rest there's "tea, tea, tea."

In late November, the inn holds a wine tasting for charity. A glittering and popular event, the very finest wines are brought out of the cellar for guests to sip.

Many guests arrive for the entire Christmas season. Chuck digs out all his great old movies, and from mid-December until the last cork has popped on New Year's Eve, the inn is full of the festive spirit: church carollers, hot cider, twinkling lights and an

incredible Nutcracker Christmas dinner complete with roast goose, sweet yams and chocolate truffles.

Then on New Year's Eve the lobby rug is rolled up and the entire place becomes a dance floor. Champagne flows and the weeks of festivities come to an elegant close.

The region surrounding the Benbow Inn is rich in history. In the winter, for many thousands of years, the Sinkyone people, one of the eleven distinct tribes in Humboldt County, inhabited the area near the Eel River. They had summer camps by the ocean in an area we now know as the Lost Coast. In 1850 they first were visited by white men in search of a direct route from the gold mines in Trinity to San Francisco. In 1914 the Northwestern Pacific Railroad was completed, making it possible for tourists to enjoy the huge redwood forests on their way to Eureka. By 1923, the Sinkyone were no more and their lands were cleared for settlement.

Curiously, it was the railroad and the development of roads into the area that were crucial in the preservation of the mammoth redwoods. The tourists who saw the trees realized that they needed to be saved from the logging that was going on full-tilt in Humboldt County. In 1918, the Save the Redwoods League was organized and to date has put into trust 155,000 acres. Because these trees flourish on moist sea air, they are found only in a narrow strip in Northern California and Southern Oregon. Their tannins resist disease; their foot-thick bark stops fire damage. Some grow to be 2,200 years old. When people speak about these giant trees, they often use religious terms, peaceful cathedrals that reach to the heavens. One place of meditation is a small structure designed by Julia Morgan, the architect who created San Simeon for William Randolph Hearst. Hearthstone is a quiet cluster of fireplaces, sheltered from the rain, but open to the forest. There you can listen to the creaking of the branches and the rustle of the wind hundreds of feet above. When you place a hand on the spongy bark of one of these trees, pause a moment. You are touching most of recorded history.

From Garberville, you can drive west through the magnificent redwoods of Richardson Grove on a little-travelled road toward Shelter Cove and the legendary Lost Coast. Good old Highway 1 couldn't quite manage this terrain, so it has remained untouched and unchanged since the days of the Sinkyone Indians. Mountains explode from the sea. From black sand beaches dotted with tidal pools, hikers can watch gray whales migrate and sea lions cavort in the surf.

Benbow Inn

445 Lake Benbow Drive
Garberville, California 95542
(707) 923–2124
Innkeepers: Patsy and Charles Watts

Butternut Squash Tortellini with Black Currant Sage Sauce

The small tortellini are made with homemade roasted red pepper pasta, a great little recipe on its own.

Tortellini
2 large red bell peppers
2 Tbl olive oil
1 egg
2 c all purpose flour
Butternut Squash and Apple Filling (recipe follows)
Black Currant Sage Sauce (recipe follows)

Place peppers on baking sheet; broil until blistered and blackened on all sides. Place in a paper bag; close tightly and allow to steam for five minutes. Rinse in cold water to remove blackened skin. Seed and *purée* with olive oil in blender or food processor. Add egg and flour; pulse until well mixed. Run machine until dough forms a ball.

Turn dough out onto floured surface; knead 8 to 10 minutes. Cover with plastic wrap; let rest for 30 minutes. Roll on floured surface until one-eighth inch thick. Cut into 20 three-inch squares.

To form tortellini: Place about a tablespoon of Butternut Squash and Apple Filling at corner of each square. Take bottom corner; fold up and over the filling, about two-thirds up the diamond. Press it into pasta. Roll the filling toward the top of the diamond while pressing the pasta on both sides of the filling to seal. Place the dough around your index finger, with filling against the nail, and pull together gently; press together. Set aside on lightly floured surface.

Bring a large pot of salted water to a boil. Drop in tortellini, a few at a time. Cook until barely tender, about four to six minutes. Drain and keep warm.

To serve, arrange tortellini on heated serving plates around a mound of steamed vegetables. Drizzle with Black Currant Sage Sauce.

Butternut Squash and Apple Filling
Make ahead of time and refrigerate until needed.

> 2 Tbl olive oil
> 1 medium yellow onion, peeled and diced
> 1 Granny Smith apple, cored and diced
> 1 Anaheim chile, seeded and diced
> 1 butternut squash, peeled, seeded and diced
> 1 tsp salt
> ½ tsp freshly ground pepper
> 2 tsp chopped fresh sage
> 1 egg
> ½ c bread crumbs

Preheat oven to 350°F.

Heat olive oil in large, ovenproof skillet. Add onion, apple, chile, squash, salt, pepper and sage; cook five or six minutes over medium-high heat. Cover with foil; bake for

30 minutes. Stir, re-cover and continue to bake for 15 minutes. Remove from oven; allow to cool. Stir in egg and breadcrumbs.

Black Currant Sage Sauce
> 1 c black currants
> 1 Tbl minced shallots
> 1 Tbl chopped fresh sage
> 2 c dry white wine
> ½ c maple syrup
> ¼ c brown sugar
> ½ c unsalted butter
> salt and freshly ground pepper to taste

In a saucepan combine currants, shallots, sage, wine, syrup and sugar. Bring to a boil over medium-high heat. Cook, uncovered, until volume is reduced to one and one-half cups. Swirl in butter; season to taste with salt and pepper.

MAKES TWO CUPS.

Pumpkin and Squash Stew with California-style Polenta

Arrange triangles of polenta in a pinwheel fashion around your serving plates. Ladle this wonderfully seasoned stew into the center.

Tomato Stock
> 1 Tbl olive oil
> 1 Tbl chopped garlic
> 1 Tbl chopped fresh basil
> ¼ c chopped parsley
> 1 tsp salt
> ½ tsp pepper
> ½ c white wine
> 6 large tomatoes, cored and chopped
> ⅓ c tomato paste
> 3 ½ c water

Heat olive oil in sauce pan and add garlic, basil, parsley salt and pepper. Cook over medium heat for one minute.

Add wine, tomatoes, tomato paste and water. Simmer for 45 minutes. Strain through fine strainer.

MAKES SIX CUPS.

Stew

>   1 lb mushrooms, sliced
>   ½ c olive oil
>   3 medium yellow onions, cut into wedges
>   3 Tbl minced garlic
>   1 Tbl ground cumin
>   1 Tbl each fresh chopped thyme,sage,oregano and
>   marjoram
>   1 tsp each grated nutmeg and cinnamon
>   ½ tsp chili powder
>   2 bay leaves
>   salt and freshly ground pepper, to taste
>   2 c (1 inch cubes) pumpkin
>   2 c (1 inch cubes) butternut squash
>   2 c (1 inch cubes) turnip
>   4 Anaheim chiles, seeded and chopped
>   1 c dry white wine
>   ¼ c maple syrup
>   3 c Tomato Stock (recipe above)
>   3 carrots, sliced diagonally
>   4 celery stalks, sliced diagonally
>   1 large red bell pepper, seeded and thinly sliced
>   1 large green bell pepper, seeded and thinly sliced
>   1 bunch cilantro, chopped
>   1 c almonds, sliced and toasted

In a large pan, *sauté* mushrooms in one-fourth cup olive oil until golden brown. Remove from pan and set aside.

Add remaining olive oil; cook onions, garlic and all spices and herbs for about five minutes. Add pumpkin, squash, turnip and chiles; cook over high heat for two minutes; stir in wine to deglaze pan. Add maple syrup, Tomato Stock; simmer for 20 minutes or until vegetables are almost tender. Add carrots and celery; continue to cook until tender, about 15 minutes. Stir in peppers and mushrooms; cook an additional three minutes. Adjust thickness of stew with Tomato Stock and season to taste.

Polenta

>   2 qt water
>   1 Tbl salt
>   2 Tbl minced garlic

>   2 c coarse yellow cornmeal
>   ½ c chopped roasted red peppers (optional)
>   8 oz mozzarella cheese, grated
>   1 c heavy cream (35%)

Combine water, salt and garlic; bring to a boil. Slowly whip in cornmeal. When polenta has thickened, add red peppers, lower heat and continue to cook, stirring constantly, for 15 to 20 minutes. Add cheese and cream; cook five minutes. Pour hot mixture onto a parchment-lined baking sheet. Cool and cut into four inch squares. Cut each square diagonally to form triangles. Arrange on serving plates, top with stew, garnish with toasted almonds and cilantro.

MAKES EIGHT TO TEN SERVINGS.

White Chocolate Ravioli Stuffed with Bittersweet Chocolate Mousse in Raspberry Sauce

Don't be intimidated by the long name of this recipe. It is a technique well worth mastering because, once learned, it is incredibly versatile. Make the dessert in three quick steps, first the mousse, then the "pasta." While they are chilling, prepare the raspberry sauce. A few minutes or even an hour before serving, assemble the ravioli.

Chocolate Mousse

>   14 oz bittersweet chocolate
>   1 tsp granulated sugar
>   1 tsp vanilla extract
>   1 Tbl Cointreau or other orange liqueur
>   3 eggs, separated
>   ¼ c heavy cream (35%)
>   4 oz chocolate, grated

Melt chocolate over simmering water until smooth. Add sugar, vanilla and Cointreau to egg yolks, beating well.

Whip cream until thickened; fold into egg mixture.

Beat egg whites until stiff; fold into egg mixture. Slowly add half the chocolate, folding in until completely incorporated. Repeat with remaining chocolate. Cover and refrigerate until set, about four hours. Garnish with grated chocolate.

White Chocolate Ravioli

18 oz white chocolate
½ c light corn syrup

Melt chocolate over simmering water, stirring until smooth. Blend in syrup, transfer to bowl, cover and refrigerate until firm, about four hours.

Knead until pliable. Divide into four pieces; roll to about one-eighth inch thick to form a rectangle. Cut out 24 circles, four inches in diameter; place two tablespoons mousse on each. Make a top with a second circle, enlarging it a bit in the center by working it with your thumbs. Place on bottom circle; seal with fork or pasta sealer.

Raspberry Sauce

2 pt fresh raspberries
granulated sugar to taste
½ c fresh mint, chopped
whole mint leaves and fresh berries for garnish

Purée raspberries and sugar until smooth; strain to remove seeds. Cover and refrigerate or use immediately.

To serve, arrange raviolis on chilled dessert plates, spoon sauce over, sprinkle with chopped mint, garnish with whole mint leaves and scatter with berries.

MAKES EIGHT TO TWELVE SERVINGS.

Pete's Poppyseed Dressing

Serve over a salad made with fresh spinach, crumbled blue cheese, a handful of seedless green grapes and topped with sliced, toasted almonds.

1 c granulated sugar
1 Tbl salt

½ c white wine vinegar
1 ¼ c vegetable oil
1 Tbl grated yellow onion
1 Tbl dry mustard
2 Tbl poppyseeds

Place sugar, salt and vinegar in saucepan; heat until sugar is dissolved. Cool, transfer to glass jar, add oil, onion, mustard and poppyseeds. Shake well. Refrigerate until needed.

MAKES ABOUT ONE PINT.

Scone Race Scones

Energetic contestants carry them around the park in the annual Scone Race. Good bears gobble them at Benson's fancy tea party!

1 ¾ c all purpose flour
¼ c granulated sugar
1 tsp salt
2 tsp baking powder
½ tsp baking soda
⅓ c unsalted butter, chilled
½ c heavy cream (18%)
¼ c orange juice
¼ c grated orange zest
½ c currants
1 egg white, beaten

Preheat oven to 350°F.

Combine flour, sugar, salt, baking powder and baking soda. Cut in butter until mixture looks like coarse crumbs. Add just enough cream and orange juice to form a soft dough. Add orange zest and currants. Turn out onto lightly floured board; roll or pat until one inch thick. With heart-shaped cookie cutter, cut out 10 to 12 scones. Place on ungreased baking sheet. Brush with beaten egg white. Bake for 15 to 20 minutes or until they begin to turn golden brown around the edges.

MAKES TEN TO TWELVE.

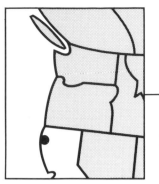

The Gingerbread Mansion

I felt like a storybook princess, living in a fanciful mansion cast back in time to a quaint hamlet of another era. Built in 1899, The Gingerbread Mansion rises three graceful stories. A delicate pink fuchsia filled with hummingbirds and flowers climbs right to the redwood eaves. Innkeeper Ken Torbert explained that to be fully dressed, a Victorian room has to have a number of crucial elements. The woodwork is all important. Capped baseboards and casements are essential. Coordinated wallpaper covers both the walls and the high ceilings from which Ken has hung "transition" lamps, lights which glow with the warmth of both gas and electricity. But The Gingerbread Mansion has far more than pretty paper and authentic trim. As the sunlight floods in, stained and leaded glass by Arcata artist Robert LeMmon sprinkles the interior with color. Both the Fountain and Gingerbread suites have twin claw-footed tubs surrounded by mirrors, perfect for his and her bubble baths. Similar deep tubs have places of honor in the other rooms with a large container of glycerine soap ready to foam into mountains of suds. Silk lampshades, lace curtains and a full complement of antique furniture make the rooms feel like Grandma's parlour.

Ken came to love old things in his student days, and when he found The Gingerbread Mansion, already a widely acclaimed piece of architecture, he filled it with furniture that would have been in a home of its day. Like such a home, there are pieces in a variety of styles artfully scattered amongst the East Lake mahogany. The most ornate is the sideboard on which afternoon tea is served. Admire its highly carved floral design while you sip orange

spice tea from an elegant bone china cup and assuage your hunger with a large helping of Harvest Apple Cake or Very Lemony Lemon Bread, the recipe that brought a first prize ribbon from Julia Child.

Breakfast begins with fresh coffee on a sideboard outside the rooms. Later there's lots of fresh fruit, warm muffins, bundt cakes and quick breads and a variety of medal-winning cheeses made at the Loleta Cheese factory from the region's dairy herds.

Before heading afield take a morning stroll through Ken's period gardens. A meandering path of French curves leads guests to hidden corners, past topiary that matches the carvings on the house and through flower beds that are planned to have six colors of bloom from February to November. It was in the rose-pink stage when I was there, with camellias dropping huge flowers all over the porch. This is the best vantage point from which to closely examine the gingerbread. The town still has craftspeople, with their original lathes, who carved the mouldings.

Ferndale calls itself "the little village that could." It sits precariously close to the San Andreas fault, amidst trembling mountains and in a river valley that is washed every decade or so by a major flood. Ferndale's citizens have proven not only that they could, but that they can, survive, flourish and create a small gem of Victoriana. The entire town, nestled between the Eel River and the Lost Coast, has been designated as a State Historical Landmark.

But it was not always so. Originally, it was the agricultural center of Northern California. Huge dairy farms surrounded the town and the magnificent ornately carved, solid redwood buildings were known as Butterfat Palaces. But both the railway and the

Patricia Brabant

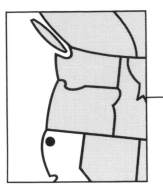

The Carter House/Hotel Carter

Behind the redwood curtain you will discover Humboldt County, a region suspended in time. At its center, alongside Humboldt Bay, is Eureka, a Victorian seaside town with a charming and singular disposition. It is a town of amazing contrasts, where hard-working loggers and counter-culture shopkeepers walk down streets lined with perfect Victorian boutiques and splashes of unbridled California art deco. Listen to any native and you will notice a distinct dialect, a special Eurekan accent where words are well-chewed, a few vowels are forgotten and others unexpectedly appear, playfully spouted into a sentence or a poem.

Coastal life is a beautiful reflection of things past. The stately, ornate mansions built by the monied lumber barons of a bygone era are once again finding their glory. Street after street is being restored. A good deal of the credit for Eureka's renaissance belongs to a sandy-haired dynamo of a man, Mark Carter, innkeeper, hotelier and builder. Born and raised in Eureka, he took his "university" education at his father's dinner table. Like the town itself, Carter is a bit of an enigma. He adores great food, vintage wines and fast cars; he has a Mercedes collection. Yet, you're as likely to find him in shirt sleeves, covered with sawdust, installing a door jamb or in an apron helping his young chefs *sauté* fresh prawns or shuck a few pails of Humboldt Bay oysters.

Mark and his wife, Christi, have created an elegant enclave of Victorian lodgings that have won accolades from everyone from *Bon Appetit* to *Motorland*. The Carter House Inn is a detailed replica of a home built in 1884 in San Francisco. The

Patricia Brabant

41

Patricia Brabant

original home was destroyed in the fire that followed San Francisco's devastating earthquake of 1906, and the plans, by Samuel and Joseph Newsom, lay mouldering until the Carters unearthed them at a Eureka antique shop. The Carters' newest addition is the self-contained Bell House with its magnificent kitchen in which guests may cook the region's specialties for themselves. Across the street is The Hotel Carter, winner of Uncle Ben's national Best Inn of the Year award in 1989. Considering that the Carter inns are hundreds of miles from any major metropolitan area, the caliber and variety of cuisine they offer is amazing. Indeed, the Carters' culinary reputation has been so widely touted that they were recently invited to cook at the highly-regarded James Beard House in New York City. Their breakfasts have been called the best in California, but although Christi's buttery pastries and freshly brewed coffee are undeniably compelling, for me dinner was the big event.

We began our meal as the last few rays of the evening sun streamed through the dining room's high windows. Spicy mustard sauce, spooned over golden cakes of shredded crabmeat, matched a lean, dry Kendall-Jackson sauvignon blanc. Fresh spinach was added just as the light oyster broth was ladled forth, creating a soup as delicious as it was beautiful. Muscovy duck breasts were grilled to perfection, bathed in a hearty zinfandel sauce—the kind you mop up with fresh bread—then surrounded with bright steamed vegetables and a head of roasted garlic. Dessert was a physical impossibility, even Christi's warm apple cobbler. There are, after all, limits on any writer's capacity for research. A tall flute of French champagne was all I could manage.

The temptation is to linger in these romantic confines, but the Redwood Region, rich with cultural interest and natural wonders, beckons one to move on to discover more of nature's secrets.

The Carter House
Hotel Carter
1033 Third Street
Eureka, California 95501
(707) 445–1390/444–8062
FAX: (707) 444–8062
Innkeepers: Mark and Christi Carter

Mark and Christi served the recipes that follow when they and their super staff brought a taste of the North Coast to the James Beard House in New York City. Enjoy.

Humboldt County Fruit Vinaigrette

Try to use the ripest fruit available. Christi says that strawberries, raspberries, nectarines or pears work well.

> *2 c large chunks of fruit (berries may be left whole)*
> *1 tsp minced dill weed*
> *1 Tbl Mendocino or other sweet mustard*
> *1 egg yolk*
> *1 ½ Tbl red wine vinegar (apple cider if using pears)*
> *juice of ½ lemon*
> *¼ c sugar*
> *1 c good quality salad oil*
> *salt and freshly ground white pepper to taste*

Purée fruit thoroughly; if seedy, pass through sieve, discard pulp, reserving *purée*.

Transfer to a large mixing bowl. Add dill, mustard, egg yolk, red wine vinegar, lemon juice and sugar. Blend to dissolve sugar.

With whisk or hand mixer on lowest speed, drizzle in oil, one-fourth cup at a time. If speed is too high, the dressing will thicken; the desired result is simply an emulsion with a slight sheen. Season to taste with salt and white pepper.

MAKES ABOUT ONE PINT.

The Chanticleer Inn
The Winchester Country Inn
The Jacksonville Inn
Tu Tu' Tun Lodge
Steamboat Inn

The Johnson House
Channel House
Flying M Ranch
Heron Haus
The Columbia Gorge Hotel

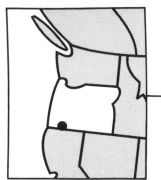

Chanticleer Inn

"Hark, Hark! I hear
The strain of strutting
Chanticleer."
—Wm. Shakespeare,
The Tempest, Act 1, Scene II

The enchanted isle in Shakespeare's *The Tempest* has powers to lift and transform the soul. So it is that Ashland, planted on what geologists believe once was the eastern shore of an island floating in prehistory, has been elevating the souls of theatrical pilgrims for most of the century.

It began with the construction of the Ashland Chatauqua Hall in 1893. Families trekked from miles around to pitch their tents under the sycamores in nearby Lithia Park, then strolled to the Chatauqua stage to be thrilled by the music of John Philip Sousa, the oratory of William Jennings Bryan and the pulpit pounding of Billy Sunday.

Although the Chatauqua died, its spirit did not; it merely changed venues. In 1935, Angus Bowmer, a teacher with a dream, coaxed the town into presenting three days of classic Shakespeare from July second to the fourth. What was once the Chatauqua Hall is now the oldest existing full-scale Elizabethan stage in the Western Hemisphere. And three days of Shakespeare have grown into the longest running festival of its type in America. The eight-month season now includes experimental drama at the Black Swan Theater, back stage tours and, of course, Shakespeare.

A short walk from the magnificent Angus Bowmer Theater is Chanticleer Inn, which takes its name from another famous pilgrimage, *The*

Canterbury Tales by Chaucer. The inn is a Craftsman Bungalow perched on a hillside overlooking the Bear Creek Valley and Cascade foothills. It's surrounded by inviting gardens piled with flowers. An old wooden swing glides on the front porch.

The open door to the kitchen lets the full aroma of roasting almonds and baking cookies permeate the inn. Each of the romantic rooms has a stack of the eleven plays which are being produced in the current year. Free-form bouquets of lilacs, or whatever innkeeper Nancy Beaver finds in bloom, fill the living areas. She and her husband Jim have adorned the walls with the works of local artists.

The living room is a cozy spot where guests mingle, chat about skiing nearby Mt. Ashland or about the evening's theatre offering while warming their toes before an open fire. Nearby, a brim-filled cookie jar beckons.

Breakfast at Chanticleer is relaxed, the food imaginative and well-prepared. Red chili corn cakes may be served with smoked salmon and roasted sweet pepper salsa. Rhubarb sour cream cake is dolloped with whipped *crème fraîche* and sprinkled with roasted hazelnuts; the cream scones are dotted with dried cranberries.

The perfect complement to Chanticleer's comfort is Chateaulin's cuisine. Located in the shadow of the Shakespeare theaters, Chateaulin Restaurant Francais is where you meet many of the town's resident actors as well as enjoy some exceptional dinners.

Chateaulin has a wonderful European ambiance.

Ray Bartholomew

It's as much a local cafe as a fine dining room. For the last 20 years co-owners Michael Donovan and David Taub have insisted on impeccable service, the freshest ingredients and classic technique in their preparation. The bread is so crusty it cracks when tapped. Michael is a local wine enthusiast, with a small, well-stocked store set up right beside the restaurant for tastings and catering. He preserves much of his inventory, including rare Oregon and California vintages, in a cool cave, dug deep into the granite hill. It's *the* place in town to purchase wine and picnic ingredients before a visit to Lithia Park. Try their duck liver *pâté*, a small baguette and some crisp vegetables to dip in a garlic-laden aioli sauce.

Summer or winter, Chanticleer and Chateaulin make a winning team. Light and airy or warm and comforting, *après* theatre or *après* ski.

Chanticleer Inn

120 Gresham Street,
Ashland, Oregon 97520
(503) 482–1919
Innkeepers: Nancy and Jim Beaver

Chateaulin Restaurant Francais

50 East Main Street
Ashland, Oregon 97520
(503) 482–2264
Co-owners: Michael Donovan and
chef David Taub

Red Chili Corn Cakes

Nancy Beaver serves these with corn kernels, hot-smoked salmon, roasted bell pepper salsa, sour cream and cilantro.

1 c cornmeal
¾ tsp chili powder
1 tsp salt
1 c boiling water
½ c milk, room temperature
1 egg, room temperature
2 Tbl melted butter
½ c all purpose flour
1 Tbl baking powder
vegetable oil as needed for frying

In medium sized mixing bowl, mix together cornmeal, chili powder, salt and boiling water. Let stand five minutes.

In separate bowl, whisk milk, egg and melted butter together; stir into cornmeal mixture. Sift flour and baking powder over batter; stir to combine. Allow batter to stand five minutes. Heat skillet over medium-high heat. Coat bottom of pan with oil. When oil is hot, spoon one-fourth to one-half cup of batter onto skillet. Cook until bubbles begin to appear on upper surface; flip and continue cooking until golden brown.

MAKES TWELVE SMALL THICK PANCAKES, FOUR SERVINGS.

Roasted Sweet Pepper Salsa

Nancy suggests, since limes have a tendency to become bitter after a few hours, that if you make the salsa in advance, add the limes at the last minute.

4 tomatoes
4 sweet peppers, a variety of colors of bell or Anaheims
2 limes, peeled and finely chopped
4 scallions, minced
1 small hot pepper, seeded and minced
½ c chopped cilantro
2 Tbl olive oil
2 Tbl vinegar
salt and freshly ground pepper to taste

Blanch tomatoes in boiling water; remove skins, chop, then place in mixing bowl. Roast peppers over burner or under broiler until skins are charred. Place in paper bag, close tightly and let stand for five minutes to steam. Peel, seed and chop; add to tomatoes with limes, scallions, hot pepper and cilantro. Stir in oil, vinegar, salt and pepper. Cover and refrigerate until ready to use. Just before serving, adjust seasonings.

MAKES TWO TO THREE CUPS DEPENDING ON SIZE OF TOMATOES.

Crabe Armoricaine

From the land of Dungeness crab comes this delicious appetizer prepared as the Bretons do. Chateaulin's Chef David Taub serves it with a crusty French bread and a crisp, dry Oregon wine such as Eyrie Vineyards 1989 Chardonnay.

3 Tbl unsalted butter
3 shallots, peeled and minced
¼ lb mushrooms, chopped
1 Tbl Cognac or brandy
3 Tbl tomato paste
½ tsp curry powder
salt and freshly ground pepper to taste
2 Tbl chopped parsley
12 oz freshly cooked Dungeness crabmeat,
    about two 1 ½ lb crabs
½ c fine bread crumbs

In a heavy skillet, melt one tablespoon of the butter over low heat; gently *sauté* shallots and mushrooms until tender. Stir in Cognac, tomato paste, curry powder, salt, pepper and parsley.

Preheat oven to 400°F. Fold in crabmeat; heap into four lightly oiled individual ramekins or real crab shells. Top with crumbs, dot with remaining butter. Bake until piping hot, about 10 to 12 minutes.

MAKES FOUR APPETIZER SERVINGS.

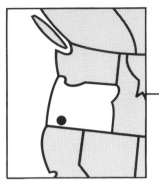

The Winchester Country Inn

Zooming around the perimeter of Crater Lake in mid-April, high in the Cascades, had been cool enough. But by the time I pulled into Ashland, the day had become sweltering, completely unspringlike. All the city gardens were exploding with color. Innkeeper Michael Gibbs greeted me, assessed the situation and quickly poured me a chilled Portland Ale. It went down like iced velvet.

He and his gracious wife Laurie are quintessential innkeepers, good natured, caring and utterly community-oriented, committed to Ashland, Oregon.

Sheltered in the lee of both the Cascade and Siskiyou mountains, the eclectic town is now home for the oldest Shakespearean festival in North America and all summer long is populated by actors, musicians and theatergoers.

The Winchester Inn began life in 1886 as the private home of Fordyce Roper, a merchant from the bay area. Because it pre-dated the railroad, its interior was Spartan; no fancy mouldings and cornices were available. In 1906 it became a hospital, but after a succession of roof fires, it was jacked up and, over three days, with the strength of one good old horse, the house was moved up the hill to its present location. "There should be a monument to that horse!" exclaims Laurie.

The food is so good that guests are interrogated by friends when they return home as to what was served at every meal. The day may begin with

Katrina Boldt

pineapple/cardamom upside-down cake or a strawberry-orange coffee cake, then proceed to some lemon-poppyseed pancakes, a lightly brandied syrup and bangers or a pair of large, perfectly poached eggs on a toasted English muffin, a layer of inn-smoked salmon underneath and bathed in dill/Dijon hollandaise.

Dinner is equally exquisite and, without question, it's the ingredients that make it so special. The freshest of greens come from a certified organic grower in nearby Talent. Laurie buys a wheel of locally produced blue cheese from the Central Point Creamery and ages it herself until it's meltingly creamy and very blue. All sorts of berries grow nearby; some, such as tayberries, are quite exotic for out-of-state visitors. In August, Laurie is able to buy a few baskets of Italian white peaches and of course there are always the famous Oregon pears, apples and hazelnuts.

After the theater or perhaps one of Michael's madcap murder mysteries, tuck yourself into bed with a little glass of Port and a truffle that cracks when you bite it, oozing buttery chocolate cream over every taste bud.

The Winchester Country Inn

35 South Second Street
Ashland, Oregon 97520
(503) 488–1113
Innkeepers: Laurie and Michael Gibbs

Cultivator Vegetable Soup

Soup is one of those easy, wonderful dishes with which gardeners can really strut their stuff.

> *1 c seeded, chopped fresh tomatoes*
> *1 medium beet, peeled and cut into small cubes*
> *½ small turnip, cubed*
> *½ rutabaga, cubed*
> *1 small onion, minced*
> *1 small zucchini, sliced thinly*
> *2 small carrots, peeled and thinly sliced*
> *1 stalk celery, diced*
> *1 tsp minced garlic*
> *1 Tbl dry sweet basil*
> *1 ½ tsp thyme*
> *1 tsp oregano*
> *vegetable stock as needed*
> *salt and freshly ground pepper to taste*
> *½ c blanched spinach, chopped*
> *6 tsp grated Parmesan cheese*

In a large soup kettle, combine the tomatoes, beet, turnip, rutabaga, onion, zucchini, carrots, celery, garlic, basil, thyme and oregano. Cover with vegetable stock; season to taste with salt and pepper. Bring to a boil over medium heat, reduce heat and simmer, covered, until vegetables are tender, about 15 to 20 minutes.

To serve, divide spinach among warm bowls, ladle soup into each and top with Parmesan cheese.

MAKES SIX GARDEN-FRESH SERVINGS.

Teng Dah Beef Filet

Michael suggests serving these with a little *wasabi* (Japanese horseradish), available in Asian food markets.

> *3 lb beef tenderloin, trimmed of fat and membrane*
> *lemon zest as needed*
> *freshly cracked black pepper as needed*

Teng Dah Marinade

⅔ c water
⅔ c light soy sauce
⅛ tsp grated nutmeg
⅛ tsp crushed anise
⅛ tsp cinnamon
2 tsp minced garlic
3 tsp grated horseradish
3 tsp freshly ground pepper
2 Tbl granulated sugar
⅓ c lemon juice.

Make diagonal slits one inch apart around the circumference of the filet. Stuff slits with a pinch of lemon zest and cracked pepper. Place in 9 x 13 inch glass pan; set aside. In a medium sized bowl, stir together water, soy sauce, nutmeg, anise, cinnamon, garlic, horseradish, pepper, sugar and lemon juice. Pour over tenderloin; cover with plastic wrap; refrigerate, turning filets every few hours, for at least eight hours, no more than 72 hours.

To serve, remove beef from marinade, reserving one cup. Cut filet into serving sized portions; broil or barbecue to desired doneness. Transfer marinade to small saucepan; bring to a boil over medium high heat. Slice cooked filets across grain and top with hot marinade.

MAKES EIGHT GENEROUS SERVINGS.

Poached Oregon Pears

You can make this dessert hours, even days, in advance.

6 ripe Oregon pears
1 c orange juice, fresh
¼ c brown sugar
¼ c Grand Marnier or other orange liqueur
½ c pineapple juice
2 tsp crushed green peppercorns
grated zest of 1 orange

Peel pears and set on end in saucepan large enough for them to stand upright. Add orange juice, brown sugar,

Grand Marnier, pineapple juice and green peppercorns. Cover and simmer, without boiling, for 90 minutes.

With slotted spoon, transfer pears to glass serving dish. Spoon liquid over them; garnish with orange zest. Chill.

MAKES SIX SERVINGS.

Fresh Oregon Fruit Terrine

Use any combination of blueberries, sliced strawberries, peeled and cubed peaches and raspberries. Laurie warns that highly acidic fruit causes the gelatin to break down.

2 tsp unflavored gelatin
1 Tbl hot water
3 egg yolks
2 Tbl sugar
½ tsp pure vanilla extract
1 c table cream (18%)
½ c milk
¼ tsp salt
1 c mixed Oregon fruit (see above)
4 c fresh or frozen strawberries
½ c heavy cream (35%)

Line 8 ½ x 4 ½ inch loaf pan with plastic wrap. Set aside.

In a small saucepan soften gelatin in hot water for five minutes. Heat gently, stirring until it becomes liquid. Meanwhile beat egg yolks with sugar until mixture forms ribbon when beaters are lifted. Whisk in vanilla, table cream, milk, salt and gelatin. Transfer to top of double boiler. Cook over simmering water until mixture reaches 165°F and coats the back of a spoon. Remove from heat. Cool. Fold fruit into cooled custard. Pour into prepared loaf pan and freeze four to six hours.

To serve, slice with serrated knife; thaw. _Purée_ the strawberries, sweetening only if necessary, and whip the cream. Spoon sauce onto serving plates. Place slices onto the berry sauce and top with cream.

MAKES EIGHT TO TEN SERVINGS.

Warren Mitchell

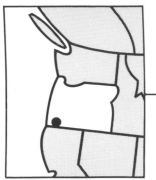

The Jacksonville Inn

It's like walking onto a set of an old western movie... a vintage stagecoach town where the horses merely have been replaced by pickup trucks. On the still night air dreams of gold and spectacular fortune are almost palpable.

Gold was discovered here in 1851, when, as legend has it, a nugget surfaced in a hoofprint in Rich Gulch Creek, and Jacksonville officially joined the ranks of other Northwest boom towns. A tent city sprang up almost overnight. Placer mining soon scarred the landscape, the richest mine being that of Chinese immigrant Gin Lin. Today the Gin Lin Trail is a perfect example of how such intense mining was performed.

After the main business district was leveled by fire in the late 1860s, brick from the Jacksonville kiln was chosen to replace the fragile frame structures. These sturdy, sometimes multi-storied buildings survived gracefully into the 20th century. The oldest, constructed in 1855, now serves as a library but once was thickly roofed with sod and served as refuge for women and children during Indian attacks. Gold shafts still run, like shadowy subterranean spiderwebs, beneath much of the old town site.

One of the mined-out shafts ends behind the mirror in the cavernous dining room of The Jacksonville Inn. The room itself has an air of history and old money. Look closely and you will see that the mortar glows in the candlelight with flecks of gold. Large servings of Oregon country cuisine reflect the seasons and the region. Marionberries may find their way into a lively vinaigrette or as a warm, sweet sauce on top of a rich *crème brûlée*. Toasted hazelnuts

Warren Mitchell

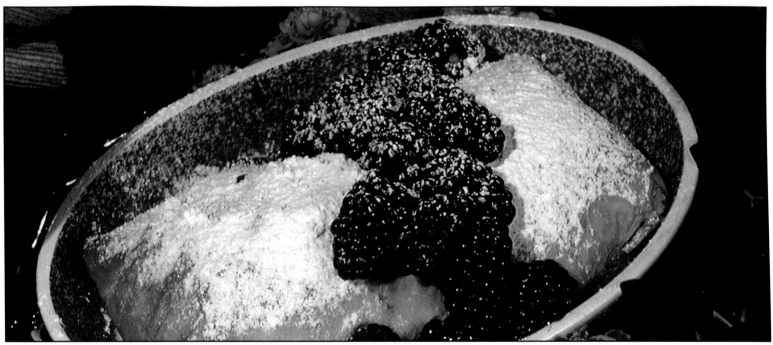

Warren Mitchell

may be ground to serve as a crispy coating for prawns or as the base for meringues heaped with fresh raspberries and sweet cream.

Reservations are essential. It took innkeeper Jerry Evans four attempts to find a table for George Bush in 1988, while Bush was campaigning for President. The food is so good that there is often a line-up into the Bistro, a more casual area and particular favorite of local businessfolk.

Breakfasts are a must, even if it's just to have coffee poured by a waitress who really cares how your day starts. These are rural people, the kind one enjoys first thing in the morning away from home.

Jerry is justifiably proud of his wine list, a compendium of 700 of some of the world's finest wines. When the mood hits, he has been known to

sell both Chateau Petrus and Lafite Rothschild by the glass. But if you crave a local wine, try a Valley View Vineyards wine. This family-run operation is just outside of Jacksonville. "Drive until you smell the feedlot and turn left," quipped a local official. Valley View vinifies one of the finest Cabernets I have tasted. Their 1987 Barrel Select won a clutch of medals. The 1990 Barrel Select Chardonnay is a sophisticated vintage with just a hint of toasted oak.

Built in 1861, The Jacksonville Inn has seen many transformations, the addition of several storeys, occupation by "ladies of the evening" and finally the ladies' removal. All the historical rooms have been completely and thoughtfully restored; a coat of fresh paint was not enough for Jerry Evans. He added every amenity a fussy traveller could ever want, from Jacuzzis and perfectly concealed audio centers to fabulous western antiques and air conditioning.

Set aside from the inn, down a quiet street, is the Honeymoon Cottage. Private and lacy, it has a steam shower, a Jacuzzi and, for honeymooners, lots of champagne.

The Jacksonville Inn

175 E. California Street
Jacksonville, Oregon 97530
(503) 899–1900
Innkeeper: Jerry Evans

Marionberry Strudel with Frangelico Custard Sauce

The combination of the Oregon fruit with the custard captures the note of rugged elegance that The Jacksonville Inn represents.

Frangelico Custard

½ c sugar
4 Tbl cornstarch
4 egg yolks
2 ½ c whipping cream, scalded
½ tsp almond extract
⅛ c Frangelico liqueur

In top of a double boiler, mix sugar, cornstarch and egg yolks. Stir in scalded cream until smooth. Cook and stir over hot water until custard is smooth and thickened.

Remove from heat. Stir in almond extract and liqueur. Place in bowl, cover with plastic film and chill before serving.

Strudel

4 c Marionberries, fresh if possible
1 ½ c sugar
½ c blackberry brandy or liqueur
4 Tbl cornstarch
½ c water
1 package phyllo dough

½ c melted butter
powdered sugar for dusting
Frangelico Custard (recipe above)

Bring Marionberries, sugar and brandy to a boil. Mix cornstarch with water and stir into berries. Stir until cornstarch is completely mixed with berries.

Cook until berry mixture turns clear and remove from heat. Cool completely. Brush layer of phyllo dough with butter and repeat with second and third layers. *Preheat oven to 350°F.* Spoon filling on end of phyllo dough, roll twice, fold ends in and roll completely. Brush lightly with butter.

Bake seam side down until golden, about 15 minutes. Dust with powdered sugar. Top with Frangelico Custard.

Carrots Jacksonville Inn

You may never want plain old steamed carrots again.

4 large carrots
2 Tbl liquid honey, slightly warmed
¼ tsp grated nutmeg
½ tsp salt
¼ tsp freshly ground pepper
¼ tsp garlic powder or minced fresh garlic
3 Tbl minced fresh parsley
1 Tbl apple juice concentrate
¼ c toasted sliced hazelnuts
¼ c clarified butter

Peel and cut carrots into large pieces; cook in small amount of boiling salted water until barely tender, about 10 to 12 minutes. Drain, cool until easy to handle; grate.

Meanwhile stir together in a small bowl the remaining ingredients, except the butter. Combine with grated carrots. Just before serving, reheat by sauteing in clarified butter for four to six minutes.

MAKES SIX SERVINGS.

Seafood Fettuccine

According to chef Diane Menzie this recipe displays the best qualities of the seafood the Pacific Northwest is famous for.

Beurre Blanc Sauce

1 c white wine
1 c white wine vinegar
5 whole peppercorns
4 tsp minced shallots
1 c whipping cream
1 c butter, room temperature

Fettuccine

2 c mushrooms, sliced
¼ c clarified butter
4 Tbl minced shallots
4 oz scallops
8 oz bay shrimp
8 steamer clams
4 mussels
12 oz fettuccine, cooked al dente
Beurre Blanc Sauce
2 green onions, minced

For sauce, bring wine, vinegar, peppercorns and shallots to a boil. Reduce by half. Add cream and reduce again by half. Turn heat to very low and whisk in butter to thicken. *Do not boil.*

Strain to remove peppercorns.

To prepare pasta, heat butter until bubbly. *Sauté* mushrooms, shallots and scallops. When scallops are almost opaque, add shrimp, clams and mussels.

Cover and continue cooking until scallops are opaque and the shrimp are warm and the shellfish are open. Add cooked pasta and toss in the pan. Add the *Beurre Blanc* Sauce to coat.

Divide to four plates; garnish with green onion.

MAKES FOUR SERVINGS.

Marionberry Crème Brûlé

An Oregonian's view of the classic French dessert.

Custard

5 egg yolks
⅓ c granulated sugar
1 ½ c whipping cream
¼ c milk
¼ tsp cinnamon

Marionberry Topping

2 c Marionberries, fresh if possible
¾ c granulated sugar
¼ c blackberry brandy
2 Tbl cornstarch
¼ c water
6 tsp brown sugar

To make the custard, whisk together egg yolks and sugar. Combine cream and milk in heavy saucepan; heat until steaming. Whisk into yolk mixture. Add cinnamon.

Preheat oven to 350°F. Divide custard equally among six lightly buttered two-thirds cup ramekins. Place in baking pan. Pour hot water into pan up to level of custard. Bake until set, about 90 minutes. Remove from water, cool and refrigerate.

Stir together berries, sugar and brandy in small saucepan. Bring to boil over medium heat. Combine cornstarch with water; stir into berries. Cook until berry mixture turns clear; remove from heat. Cool completely. Pass through food mill or strainer to remove seeds. Hold sauce until ready to serve. To serve, rewarm sauce.

Preheat broiler.

Arrange custards on baking sheet; sprinkle each with a teaspoon of brown sugar. Broil until sugar melts and bubbles. Spoon warm sauce over custards and serve immediately.

MAKES SIX SERVINGS.

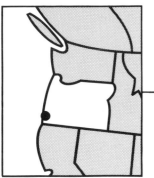

Tu Tu' Tun Lodge

"Just checkin' in?" queried a bathrobe-encased guest on his way to the pool. "Yes," I replied a bit wearily. "You're going to just love it. This place is great!" And off he trotted. No one could've said it better.

I unlocked the door to Bigfish Riffle and outside, beyond the nasturtium lined balcony, a large kingfisher took off with a flourish. At least a dozen hawks were circling, scanning the wide Rogue River for a steelhead snack. A jet boat loaded with thrill seekers headed slowly upstream; meanwhile, a loud splash resounded from the pool—could it have been my neighbour?

Bigfish Riffle, my home for the next few days, was named after a fast flowing, shallow section of the river, much like a baby rapid, where mail boat driver Fred Lowery caught a large Chinook. Naturally the size of the salmon has increased over the years. Other rooms are named because of timeworn river tales. Bony Point was where the water opened up some native graves; Lobster Creek is a favorite crayfish hole; and at Coal Riffle a barge tipped, emptying its contents into the fish filled waters. That accident prompted a ban on coal mining on the Rogue.

After a long day, everybody was hungry and thirsty—dinner was both extraordinary and filling, but did not end the evening. Guests slowly filtered outside, carrying coffee and brandies. As dusk deepened, we sat overlooking the river and chatted. Sparks floated into the night.

Faith Echtermeyer

59

Inside a lively pool game began. A guest from New York City had pumped up the player piano and was cranking out "An American in Paris." Others had found the card table. Some had headed back to the privacy of their decks to sit by the fire, outlined with slate tiles the color of the river water, or to float outdoors in their "moon-soaker" tubs.

Tu Tu' Tun (pronounced "to-TOOT-in") means "people by the river." Dirk and Laurie Van Zante operate the inn with the help of their children, Drake and Kyrsten. Dirk discovered that the site on which the lodge sits was an old camping place for the Tu Tu' Tuni Indians, a sub-tribe of the Rogue River Indians. Dirk, a trained biologist, has found arrowheads, blackened cooking stones, bones and shells.

It would be difficult not to enjoy the Van Zante

kids. They love nature almost as much as their parents do. If guests come back without river fish in their creel, Drake takes them to Libby Pond. The trout they catch are next morning's breakfast. He is constantly rescuing baby birds and Laurie proudly points out that dozens of swallows have survived because of Drake's gentle care and Science Diet.

As Laurie explains, Drake understands his role and relishes it. Basically he shares his life-style with the children of guests. He takes them in his little boat to see the beaver dam or gets them to help him catch a digger squirrel with his Have-a-Heart trap. He may be in the midst of transporting fish from a drying creek to the river or nursing another set of baby birds to flight. Kyrsten, three years younger than Drake, gravitates towards the daughters of guests. She takes them swimming and cycling and shows them how to

61

Steamboat Inn

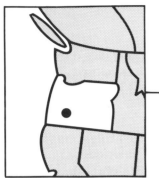

For well over half a century, well-known fisher-folk like Zane Grey and countless less famous anglers have journeyed to cast their lines into the legendary North Umpqua River. The history of fly-fishing and of Steamboat Inn are totally intertwined. Indeed, they remain so today.

The green-butted skunk was invented at Steamboat Inn by Dan Callaghan; in fact the famous skunk itself—the original one without the green butt—was created by Mildred Krogel, a resident of the area. Then there are the Cummings, and the Golden Demon, the Purple Peril and the Umpqua Special. All are steelhead flies and all have been written into the lore of the North Umpqua River and of Steamboat Inn.

But Steamboat Inn, as firmly fixed on the rocky bank as the fir trees that surround it, is far more than fly-fishing. It is a paradise set in the middle of the huge Umpqua National Forest on a road that winds along the river's edge through majestic evergreen trees.

Pick up a map, order a picnic lunch and set out for a hike that could last for an hour or a day. The trails that are woven through the forests take you past deep pools, down wildflower, fern-filled paths and even up to an old homestead site. The river is fed by many tiny streams full of perfect swimming holes. Both Canton and Steamboat Creeks have waterfalls to frolic beneath. There is one hard-to-find place where the river fans out over flat stones creating a myriad of chutes. From late June through early September, summer sun drenches the area, making it the perfect place to picnic and play in the cascades of crystalline water.

Many guests come in early spring specifically to photograph wildflowers. Up river, along the Mott Trail, the woods and meadows are full of snowy trilliums, rich blue larkspur, fragrant violets and banks of wild lilacs. The ledges below the inn are painted pale yellow by lambs tongue.

Relax, resting your trail-worn feet, on the sweeping porch above the river or in the library in front of the dancing fire. This comfortable common room houses the Van Loan's eclectic collection of books along with a small selection of videos and books on tape. One can also browse through the inn's shop which provides a showcase for regional flies, handmade rods, interesting artwork and the extras that most guests know they need or have always wanted.

The Van Loans, with Steamboat's manager, Pat Lee, run the Lodge to reflect a relaxed style. Dinners are served, 30 minutes after last light, on a one-foot-thick sugar pine table. Everything that can be made at the inn, is. The bread may be a moist and crunchy walnut-onion or spicy cornmeal. Salads with lots of fresh herbs come from the inn's gardens. Sharon is even attempting to cultivate shiitake mushrooms. The menu is fixed, with enough variation to keep the fussiest person happy.

Quite frankly, my mouth waters as I recall the dinner I ate at Steamboat. Fresh, thickly sliced tomatoes lay on a bed of spinach from the garden, doused with a pungent basil vinaigrette. Baskets were filled and refilled with the day's fresh bread, an

herbed sourdough. Flank steak was barbecued to rare perfection, carrots lightly steamed in wine until they were still a bit crisp, then gently simmered in a honey-mustard sauce—enough to satisfy the largest appetite. Had I been out on the river all day, there would have been some justification for having a second helping of soy-sesame potatoes.

The desserts at Steamboat are as good as the *entrées*. Some are old-fashioned, like the rhubarb upside-down cake, while others, like the walnut roulade with chocolate and fresh strawberries, are quite contemporary. By the end of the evening, new friendships had been forged over satisfying food, plentiful Oregon wine and richly brewed coffee.

After you've hiked the trails, swum the streams and visited the waterfalls, you can also explore old logging roads, take a leisurely tour of local wineries, hunt for the area's half-dozen covered bridges, raft a whitewater river (from November to June) or best of all, catch a flashing silver steelhead!

The mark of a great inn is that guests may do as little or as much as they choose. At Steamboat, one can simply rest by the rushing river, meditating on the utter beauty of the area.

Steamboat Inn

Steamboat, Oregon 97447–9703
(503) 498–2411 or (503) 496–3495
FAX: (503) 498–2411 *2
Innkeepers: Sharon and Jim Van Loan
Manager: Patricia Lee

Ron Fraese

Baked Asian Pears

The pears and prunes make an interesting and unusual flavor combination along with the lemon, brandy and nutmeg.

>   12 dried prunes
>   1 slice lemon
>   ½ cinnamon stick
>   ½ c water
>   1 c dry white wine
>   3 plump Asian pears, halved and cored
>   2 Tbl melted butter
>   2 Tbl raw sugar
>   ½ tsp freshly grated nutmeg
>   3 Tbl brandy
>   water, as needed
>   lemon balm leaves and rose geranium flowers as
>   garnish

In a heavy saucepan, cook prunes, lemon slice, cinnamon stick, water and wine until prunes are tender, about 30 minutes. Set aside.

Preheat oven to 350°F. Arrange pears, cut side down, in a shallow 9 x 13 inch baking dish. Drizzle with melted butter, sprinkle with sugar and nutmeg. Add brandy and enough water to cover the bottom of the pan. Bake for 40 minutes or until tender. Prick pears thoroughly several times during the baking period. Add liquid as needed to keep bottom of pan covered.

Serve warm or at room temperature in dessert dishes, cut side up. Fill indentations with two prunes each; then spoon pan liquid over pears. Garnish with lemon balm and rose geranium flower.

MAKES SIX SERVINGS.

Potato Pancakes with Lemon Thyme

This variation on a classic dish features lemon thyme freshly picked from The Johnson House's herb garden.

2 large russet potatoes
½ yellow onion
2 eggs, slightly beaten
2 Tbl all purpose flour
½ tsp freshly grated nutmeg
¼ tsp freshly ground white pepper
½ tsp salt
½ tsp minced fresh lemon thyme
¼–⅓ c unsalted butter

Using a Mouli or other hand grater, shred potatoes and onion. Put into dish towel; twist and squeeze tightly to remove as much liquid as possible. Transfer to mixing bowl and stir in eggs, flour, nutmeg, pepper, salt, and lemon thyme.

Preheat oven to 150°F. In a heavy skillet, melt a spoonful of butter until it foams. Drop small mounds of potato mixture into skillet and with spatula, shape into flat circles about three inches in diameter and one-half inch thick. Fry until undersides are golden brown. Flip and continue to cook, pressing down from time to time with spatula until golden, about four to six minutes. Keep warm in oven on cake rack. Add additional butter for each batch.

Serve on warmed plates with applesauce and *crème fraîche*. Garnish with small sprigs of lemon thyme.

Makes six servings.

Wild Mushroom Cheese Soufflé

Pine mushrooms are almost as valuable as gold. Jayne's forager makes certain that The Johnson House can frequently serve them in this fabulous *soufflé*. Jayne notes, however, that dried *shiitake* mushrooms work well; simply reconstitute them and use as directed.

7 large eggs
¼ c unsalted butter
¼ c all purpose flour
½ tsp salt
¼ tsp freshly ground white pepper
⅛ tsp freshly grated nutmeg
⅛ tsp cayenne pepper
2 c milk, scalded
2 tsp cornstarch
1 Tbl water
½ c finely grated Parmesan cheese
¾ c coarsely shredded Gruyère cheese
6 large wild mushrooms, sliced thinly, about 2 c
1 tsp minced fresh rosemary

Separate eggs; place whites in large mixing bowl; set aside.

In heavy saucepan, melt three tablespoons of the butter; stir in flour. Cook until bubbling over medium heat. Whisk in salt, pepper, nutmeg, cayenne and scalded milk. Cook, stirring constantly, until thickened, about five minutes.

Blend cornstarch with water; whisk into hot mixture. Remove from heat; vigorously whisk in egg yolks. Add Parmesan cheese and transfer to another large mixing bowl.

Melt remaining butter in skillet over medium high heat. Toss in mushrooms and rosemary. *Sauté* until beginning to brown. Set aside.

Beat egg whites until very stiff. Gently fold half into cooked mixture. Sprinkle with shredded cheese, then fold in remaining whites until completely incorporated.

Preheat oven to 375°F. Spoon half this mixture into six lightly oiled or buttered ramekins. Divide mushrooms among dishes. Top with remaining soufflé mixture.

Bake for 20 minutes or until evenly browned on top. Serve immediately.

Makes six servings.

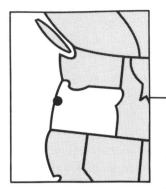

Channel House

Channel House hangs over the inlet at Depoe Bay, the smallest natural harbor in the world. Using the binoculars that Channel House has supplied in each guest room, you can watch whales play in the kelp beds right from your room, or better still, from your private outdoor whirlpool while sipping a glass of champagne.

Be careful though—on special days, even on Main Street, you could get drenched by a whale spouting too close to shore. Nevertheless, be sure to go for a walk to get a close look at the narrows.

This turbulent water, bracketed by ancient lava pillows, forms a thin, yet awesome, connection between the bay and the Pacific Ocean. Seals surf onto the seaweed draped rocks just below the inn. Diving birds bob about for a while, then quickly disappear as a flash of silver streaks beneath the surface. The local coast guard detachment often frightens casual passers-by with their search and rescue maneuvers which they execute in the surging tidal flow under the bridge.

As the rollers subside and low tide nears, kids and adults fish for ugly, albeit delicious, cabezon and spirited sea bass. Most return with long stringers of flopping seafood.

Few inns are so close to both whale watching tours and fishing charters. Just walk across the bridge. Although salmon is the most common gamefish, daily charters run out of Depoe Bay in search of halibut, the giant flatfish that swim at a depth of 180–600 feet. At the end of the summer, charters head up to 80 miles offshore to fish for the feisty albacore tuna.

"Depoe" was the chosen English name of Siletz Indian Chief White Buffalo Robe. In 1867, he was ceded 200 acres around the small inlet which soon carried his name. This area was rich in native life: The shoreline is dotted with middens, the remnants of great feasts. By the late 1920s a graceful bridge had been constructed across the bay and a rough, but passable, coast highway had been built. Tourism began.

In the 1940s the present bridge was built, and at its base brave souls boarded boats to head into the Pacific to deep-sea fish. Somewhere nearby a young city slicker was attempting to become a sport-fishing guide. Although he never did make his fortune, the late Stan Allyn became beloved in Depoe Bay for his colorful story-telling. If you enjoy homespun writing at its personal best, search out his small paperbacks and head to Channel House for an evening's reading.

In the morning, enjoy a wonderfully satisfying breakfast in the breakfast room. When you've finished, you'll be tempted to return to your cozy room. However, don't forget the location of Channel House makes it possible to venture out to experience all that the Oregon Coast has to offer. And it has plenty. Try deep sea fishing, whale watching or just walking by the ocean. For dinner, depend on the staff of Channel House to make recommendations and reservations.

The Oregon Coast Council for the Arts sponsors live theater, displays, festivals and workshops from Tillamook to Newport, where a new Performing Arts

Carl L. Finseth

Center regularly features plays. Newport, an easy 30 minute drive from Depoe Bay, is also home to the Oregon Coast Ballet Company.

On the south shore of Yaquina Bay, you'll find the Oregon Coast Aquarium. Situated on 29 acres of typical coastline, complete with caves and tidepools, visitors can come face-to-tentacle with giant Pacific octopus, watch frisky sea otters and tufted puffins. Inside the four galleries, there's Discovery Bay, where youngsters are encouraged to put their hands into a box to touch real sea creatures and then open the lid to discover the animal's identity.

Coastal hikes are in abundance around Depoe Bay. Fogarty Creek State Park and Boiler Bay lie north of town, and Cape Foulweather, so named by Captain James Cook because of the gales he and his crew encountered, is a mile to the south.

Hikers will encounter the remains of the steam schooner, *J Marhoffer*, which ran aground in 1910; a myriad of tidepooling opportunities; Yaquina Head lighthouse and many colonies of nesting sea-birds, from common gulls to cormorants and murres.

Channel House

Box 56
35 Ellingson St.
Depoe Bay, Oregon 97341
(503) 765–2140/(800) 447–2140
FAX: (503) 765–2191
Innkeepers: William "Kam" Mix and Carl Finseth

71

Blueberry Popovers with Creamy Lemon Sauce

Use special popover pans for this recipe. They are deeper than muffin tins.

5 Tbl butter
3 eggs
1 ½ c milk
1 ½ c all purpose flour
½ tsp salt
½ c blueberries
Creamy Lemon Sauce (recipe follows)

Preheat oven to 400°F.

Place one teaspoon butter in each of six popover pans. Set aside.

In large bowl, whisk eggs till foamy. Beat in milk, flour and salt. Melt remaining butter; whisk into batter.

Place popover pans into oven until butter is melted and bubbling. Remove and fill three-fourths full with batter. Spoon blueberries onto batter. Bake for 10 minutes; reduce heat to 350°F and continue to bake for an additional 30 minutes.

MAKES SIX SERVINGS.

Creamy Lemon Sauce

Although this is used as a breakfast sauce at Channel House, it is wonderful poured over fresh fruit for dessert.

1 egg
1 c granulated sugar
juice of 2 lemons
3 Tbl butter
1 c heavy cream (35%)

In a small saucepan whisk together egg, sugar and juice. Cook over low heat, whisking constantly, until creamy. Stir in butter a bit at a time.

Cool and refrigerate if not using immediately.

Just before serving, beat cream until stiff. Fold in lemon mixture. Serve over Blueberry Popovers.

MAKES ONE AND ONE-HALF CUPS SAUCE.

Spicy Oven Omelette with Chile Cheese Sauce

Omelette
18 eggs
1 c sour cream
1 c milk
1 c cottage cheese
1 (4 oz). jar pimentos, drained and chopped
½ c diced green chiles
1 c shredded Monterey Jack cheese
2 Tbl butter

Chile Cheese Sauce
3 Tbl butter
3 Tbl all purpose flour
1 c milk
1 c shredded smokey cheddar cheese
¼ c diced green chiles

Preheat oven to 350°F.

Whisk or blend together eggs, sour cream, milk and cottage cheese. Stir in pimentos, chiles and cheese.

Place one tablespoon butter into each of two nine-inch round glass cake pans. Melt in oven. Pour egg mixture into pans; bake for 45 minutes or until firm and golden. Cool for 10 minutes before slicing and serving. While omelette is baking make the sauce. Melt butter in heavy saucepan over medium heat. Stir in flour; let bubble for 30 seconds. Whisk in milk, cooking until thickened. Stir in cheese and chiles. Serve over omelette wedges.

MAKES TWELVE SERVINGS.

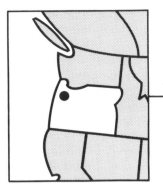

Flying M Ranch

The welcome I received at Flying M was as warm and genuine as it could be. Eleanor Mitchell, all smiles and grace in her polished cotton dress and hand-crocheted collar, looked completely appropriate to the setting, that is, until she stepped out from behind the counter to reveal her neatly tied running shoes.

Quietly, with old-fashioned country eloquence, Eleanor began to recount her family history. She and her brother Bryce grew up on the property that now is part of Flying M Ranch, "right out there on the meadow where the airstrip is." Their parents cleared the stumps by pulling them with a second-hand Allis Chalmers Model B or blasted them out. "It's a wonder we're still here. It was old dynamite and we put the sticks under the stumps. We could've been blown to heck."

In the early days Iva and Clarence "C.B." Mitchell had a huge garden irrigated by roadside ditches. "Mom felt if she didn't put up 100 quarts of everything, we wouldn't make it through the winter. Peas, beans, squash, carrots. We'd dig potatoes and buy fruit from the valley. The last time we picked any real quantity of blackberries was after the 1939 Tillamook burn; that year there was a prolific crop. We'd swap vegetables back and forth with our friends. They're second and third generaton friends now, between children and grandchildren. We still know 'em and they're still very dear."

The house in which she and Bryce were born was next to a stage line, a comfortable stop for hunters and fishermen heading into the hills or further on to Tillamook. It had been a hotel, built

Doreen L. Wynja

73

Doreen L. Wynja

from lumber milled on the site. It was a wonderful roomy place for kids to grow up. "And there was a great big maple tree for us to play under in the front yard." The hotel had been built by the Petch family in the 1880s. Mrs. Petch, the first hotelier, was shot to death by a competitor whose small inn stood just beyond the river crossing. At that point, the ownership of the hotel reverted to a timber company. High in the mountains, Iva and C. B. Mitchell looked down at the sunny valley. Their home in the hills where they had settled was "wintery and disagreeable" and they longed for the warmth of the valley. In 1921, they purchased the Petch Place along with 80 acres, a mill pond and a splash dam used to propel logs down the river to Carlton. It was the era of oxen teams and skid roads, but rail lines were quickly being built up the mountain. The low-geared tractor hauled the timber down the steep incline. There were some horrendous accidents. High geared engines would take over at the railhead to haul the load the final ten miles to Carlton. It was also an era of uncontrollable forest fires. Scars from the second Tillamook burn can still be seen. Flames leapt from treetop to treetop across 311,000 acres of old growth forest. The Mitchells went up the mountain in their old car to check the fire's progress. "We could hear the roar," recalls Eleanor. High, dry winds lit new fires so quickly that they were forced to drive through an inferno on their way home.

Eleanor went to work in town while Bryce went to school. There weren't enough kids to keep the old schoolhouse going and so the hillbilly kids were bussed to Yamhill. It was then Bryce found that pulling a cute little girl's pigtails was fun. "He says he did it because I was the only one that blushed," quips Barbara. And that was the beginning of Bryce and Barbara Mitchell's long relationship.

When they were married, they went through much of the same hard mountain life that their logger parents had faced. Barb would leap about the fallen logs, setting chokers and driving cat with the best of them. They shot much of their meat and began to build their dream, a guest ranch at the foot of Trask Mountain.

In 1971 the original log lodge was completed. Daughters Brenda and Beth moved home and it became, as Bryce had once mused, a place where their family could make a living off their land.

A little more than a decade later, a tragic fire decimated the main lodge. But strength and determination run hot in Mitchell blood. With the help of family and many loyal friends, they built the lodge that stands today. By January 1985, the new lodge opened.

The meals, like many of the people who eat them, are hearty and homespun. This is the food that has kept the country going. Many people fly in to eat. It's not uncommon to see more parked planes than cars and 4x4s. Well-scrubbed ranchers, many tanned the color of leather, and holidaying city-folk all congregate from breakfast right through until midnight. Each day while I was there, Ben Rushford, a semi-retired dentist from Portland, flew in a different set of friends just for the mammoth, farm-style breakfast. Sausage, ham and bacon go with the eggs, home-fried potatoes, biscuits and gravy. Links of sausage and scrambled eggs are wrapped in flapjacks, dusted with sugar and served with syrup. There are even sirloin steaks, and of course, Jean Belanger's fabulous cinnamon rolls.

By the time breakfast is finished, lunch is beginning. I don't think I'll ever forget the wide-eyed astonishment when a young visitor faced his first ranch burger with its mountain of freshly cut fries and plate-sized bun. The Beef Heater is the type of meal a true wrangler would eat, grilled roast beef topped with Tillamook cheddar and sweet chiles on Jean's freshly baked sourdough bread.

The dinner menu tends to be a bit more exotic. The locals can eat beef every day of the week. They come here for dishes like Cajun Fettuccine or Baked Brie Cheese served with apples and roasted garlic. Visitors regularly enjoy baby back ribs, old-fashioned country fried steak or the Trask Mountain fillet, set on a bed of freshy steamed spinach. You won't find any arugula in your salads here, just crisp lettuce and generously poured ranch-made dressings. Finish, if you can, with a warm-from-the-oven cobbler made with Ione Cook's boysenberries, a cream-filled chocolate eclair or one of the lodge's five-inch-high pies. "I never eat like this!" is a common comment heard throughout the dining room.

Bryce Mitchell is a towering man. He would be quite intimidating if he didn't have such a warm smile and welcoming handshake. It's rare that he sits down, but when he does, there's usually a grandchild on his knee. Few men work as physically hard as he does. Building roads, felling trees for new buildings and doing the heavy maintenance that such a ranch requires all fall under his domain. When the flames blackened their original rock-faced fireplace, he and Barbara took their old '57 Dodge flatbed truck to eastern Oregon, rolled boulders down a hill and, with a splitting mall, "busted up 35 tons of face rock."

Climbing up Trask Mountain to the upper cabin, you'll travel over miles of Bryce's crushed gravel roads, past Cougar Springs, and telephone poles C.B. Mitchell cut decades ago. Spectacular vistas flow to the mountainous horizon. Bryce can point out places where elk calves frolic on the earth banks, sometimes trampling newly planted trees.

The summit, with its wood-heated cabin and

outdoor shower (I checked and the water *is* hot!) is the destination of many of the overnight trail rides. The horses the Mitchells have chosen over the years are calm and strong, perfect for packing into the hills. In both winter and summer, riders are met by cooks from the ranch, who barbecue steaks, finish the smokey baked beans, whip up a batch of "Bullfrog," bake Barb's fluffy rolls and dish out great country desserts. As a family, this is where they have their traditional Thanksgiving celebration, a turkey roasted on a spit.

Trask Mountain, indeed all of Flying M Ranch, is an elemental place. Black bears, bobcats, the odd cougar, raccoons and coyotes roam the forest. Hawks and one pair of eagles soar on the updrafts over the canyons.

It's a place where the small cabin, complete with roses, champagne and a two person whirlpool is totally unexpected. The river courses along just below the cabin's private deck. Other rooms are more utilitarian. Nothing fancy, but clean as a whistle. No matter what accommodation you choose, though, I guarantee that it will include a mammoth portion of country hospitality. You will surely meet Barb and Eleanor, perhaps Brenda and Beth; you may hear young Mitchell bugling for elk. But if you don't have a chance to meet Bryce, don't be too surprised. He's probably off on some mountain, building another road.

Flying M Ranch

23029 N.W. Flying M Road
Yamhill, Oregon 97148
(503) 662–3222
FAX: (503) 662–3202
Innkeepers: Bryce and Barbara Mitchell

Oregon Wine and Onion Soup

The secret to this soup is to use lots and lots of onions, the more varieties the better. And Oregon pinot noir is an absolute must. A glass for the cook, a splash for the soup.

> *½ c butter*
> *6 c sliced or julienned onions*
> *1–2 leeks, cleaned and finely sliced*
> *2–3 garlic cloves, minced*
> *5 c chicken stock*
> *3 c beef stock*
> *2 tsp Worcestershire sauce*
> *⅛ tsp ground cloves*
> *1 c Oregon pinot noir*
> *salt and freshly ground pepper to taste*
> *minced green onions as garnish*

Melt butter in large saucepot. Add onions, leeks and garlic; *sauté* over medium-low heat until tender and caramel-brown. Stir in chicken and beef stock, Worcestershire, cloves and pinot noir. Season to taste with salt and pepper. Cover and simmer for 15 to 20 minutes. Ladle into heated soup bowls. Garnish with minced green onions and serve with a great crusty bread, preferably as good as Barb's sourdough loaves.

MAKES SIX TO EIGHT SERVINGS.

Oregon Crawfish Boil

With a typically wry sense of country humor, it was called a "Craw-Dad Boil" on Father's Day.

> *16 c water*
> *2 star anise*
> *3 bay leaves*
> *5 whole cloves*
> *½ cinnamon stick*
> *2 juniper berries*
> *½ large carrot, coarsely chopped*
> *1 c dry white wine*
> *juice of 1 lemon*
> *3–5 lb live crawfish*

84

opened the Warren Packing Company, one of the original coastal salmon canneries. The empire might have been even greater had Warren's father, the founder of the cannery, not been aboard the *Titanic* in 1912.

Heron Haus sits high on a residential hill thickly covered with ivy. High hedges camouflage the driveway and a country-style orchard.

Enormous rhododendrons form a perfect background, surrounding a swimming pool which sparkles in the early morning summer sunlight. Indoors, it is three stories of classical elegance. Duvets cover multi-pillowed beds.

The original plumbing, installed by a creative craftsman, features a shower with seven showerheads. On an original sleeping porch a spa has been added, allowing guests to relax while enjoying the panoramic view.

On the third floor is a suite that stretches across the west side of the house. This quiet, secluded retreat is a delightful hideaway in a busy city.

The old mansion is warm and friendly. Its halls are filled with family photos and treasures including such prizes as the gold medal Julie's athletic son won with his record swim in the Pan Am Games. It's also scattered with her own and her parents' artifacts. An ancient shell from South Dakota shines with a glint of bronze. A miniature grouping of tiny woven baskets, the true test of a native weaver's art, is a priceless gift from Margaret Mead's husband to Julie's mother.

As I finished my coffee, music floated into the plant-filled conservatory, keeping time with the rain

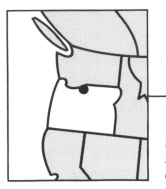

The Columbia Gorge Hotel

"Most popular summer resort of the Middle Columbia River; it offers the happy combination of rest and quiet— the sweetness and light—and pure, exhilarating mountain air. Here, in the foreground, winds the majestic Columbia. Across this historic stream is the state of Washington. Towering high over its neighboring peaks is Mount Adams, crowned centuries since with a 'diadem of snow' 12,224 feet above the level of the seas; in the opposite direction—to the south 27 miles—Mount Hood rears its lofty head 11,225 feet, its torso clothed in the raiment of cloudlets; its peak like a crystal zone set into a background of ethereal azure, the eternal symbol of the heavens of every creed on earth. On the east and the west are the forest-clad foothills of the Cascades."

This turn of the century advertisement with all its syrupy adjectives was praising the merits of early Hood River. The setting is still indeed grand but today's Hood River is a town riding high on the fabulous winds that funnel up, and later down, the Columbia River. It is the wind-surfing capital of the planet and an outdoor-lovers' paradise.

Surrounded by the extraordinary natural beauty of the Columbia Gorge, native life on the river flourished for almost 10,000 years. It was known as a "land for all seasons," and an estimated 22,000 souls lived on the banks from The Dalles to the river's mouth. A particularly striking lookout stood on the edge of a cliff in a thick grove of trees. A narrow rivulet tumbled 207 feet over its edge. The natives called the creek "Wah-gwin-gwin," meaning "rushing water."

In 1792, the area was explored by Captain Robert Gray on his ship *Columbia*. A little more than a decade later, President Thomas Jefferson sent Captain Meriwether Lewis and his friend William Clark on their legendary cross-continent trek. In 1805 they described the site where the town of Hood River now stands, naming the tributary after Francis Labeasche, a private who had killed three ducks that morning in the marshy area at the river's mouth. On the cliff top there were four native houses, built with alder frames and cedar bark roofs.

This part of the river, from Hood River to Portland, was the end of the Oregon Trail. In 1843 nearly 900 settlers had walked the 2,000 mile length. By 1849, about 11,500 pioneers had made it to Oregon by raft, canoe, pack train and on foot.

Dog River was the early settlers' name for the Labeasche. But when Nathaniel Coe began farming the area in 1854, Mrs. Coe changed the name to Hood River. By 1884, the town of Hood River had been laid out and incorporated, complete with deeds that had whiskey restrictions as a legal rider.

The stately site on which The Columbia Gorge Hotel now stands was originally developed in 1904 by Bobby Rand, a Hood River pioneer, as the Waw Gwin Gwin Hotel. According to Rand, the tradition of hospitality went back for many centuries on that site. "This used to be a great meeting place for the Indians in the early days....I was taken up by John Dye and his squaw. I bought it from a man named Amen and paid twenty-eight hundred dollars for forty-three acres. People thought that I was an easy mark to pay that amount for forty-three acres of rocks and oak trees stretched along the bluffs which overlooked the Columbia. They didn't know that sunsets and waterfalls, rugged old oaks and huge heaps of weatherworn rocks had any commercial value, but for every nickel I put into this place, I will take a dollar out."

92

Those were the days of steamers plying the waters from the Cascades to The Dalles. To alert the hotel, the captain would sound the whistle once for each guest he had on board. Maids would then quickly make up the appropriate number of beds.

In 1920, Rand and his family sold their interests to lumber baron Simon Benson. He had just helped to complete what many of the era claimed to be the world's most beautiful road, the Columbia Gorge Scenic Highway, from Hood River to Portland. Benson's dream was to create an utterly opulent hotel for travellers at the end of this road. He hired some of the Italian stone masons that had built the highway to embellish his hotel.

The inn had barely opened before it had an international reputation. Presidents Roosevelt and Coolidge, actresses Myrna Loy and Jane Powell and, rumor has it, even Rudolph Valentino have graced the hotel.

As they did with most palatial establishments, the depression and the ensuing war took their toll on the hotel. After a number of changes in ownership, Boyd Graves bought it in 1981. He, like Simon Benson, is an expansive man with fine taste. He loves his old hotel. Outdoors on a warm summer night he walks about chuckling with happiness. He stops to chat with a pair of retired firemen who are busy estimating the height of the waterfall in relation to the ladder length on their pumper trucks. Graves revels in the hotel business, from marathon tasting sessions in the kitchen with the chefs to coaching young people in the art of hospitality. As a result, The Columbia Gorge Hotel runs like a perfectly tuned clock.

The dining room is elegant. Starched uniforms, gracious service, polished candelabra, and a grand piano are part of the scene.

The appetizers are excellent, a touch of Oregon with lots of California inspiration. Dungeness crab cakes are light and creamy with a celery root salad and ancho chile sauce. The crust on the smoked salmon pizza is thin, crisp and full of flavor, a counterpoint to the mellow, cool salmon, crunchy caviar and tempura battered onion rings. With a flourish, the server flames the dressing for the spinach salad and tosses it with applewood smoked duck breast.

One in your party must order the broiled ahi. Ahi is not a Northwest fish, but the sesame crust of this presentation and chile oil sauce are superb. For dessert, try the apple tart "Columbia Gorge" made with caramel-sauced Hood River apples on a sweet puff pastry. Then relax in the lounge with a little brandy, listen to the piano and forget everything outside of those four walls.

The Columbia Gorge Hotel sits in the heart of the Columbia River Gorge National Scenic Area with many natural and man-made wonders a short drive away. Your stay at the hotel could include short trips to any of the following: the majestic Multnomah Falls; the Bonneville Dam, fish ladder and hatchery; Maryhill Museum with its surprising Rodin collection; Mt. Hood for year-round skiing; an afternoon of winery hopping; a day or two of golf at any of the several nearby courses; or just watching the butterfly-like windsurfers as they frolic on the waves of the mighty Columbia.

The Columbia Gorge Hotel

4000 Westcliff Drive
Hood River, Oregon 97031
(800) 345–1921
FAX: (503) 386–3359
Innkeeper: Patrick J. Halloran

The Shelburne Inn
Haus Rohrbach Pension

The Captain Whidbey Inn
Turtleback Farm Inn

Doug Plummer

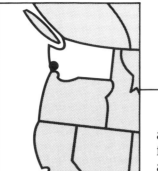

The Shelburne Inn

It was early November, after a storm. The rain had fallen in curtains, driving against the mainland, soaking the mossy forests. The sea, ragged and torn, foamed white with colliding waves, exploding in every direction. Suddenly, the sun broke through, transforming the wet sand into rippled glass, mirroring a bewhiskered, dancing innkeeper, replete in stained yellow rainslicks, shovel in hand.

From the time he was a kid, David Campiche has pounded that wide expanse of beach in a strange shellfish shuffle, searching for the fat, elusive and lightning quick razor clam. He is a gourmet, and from the kitchen at The Shelburne Inn guests experience clams and oysters in ways of which they have never dreamed.

Willapa Bay, with the most famous oyster beds in the Northwest, is just down the road a few miles. There oysters are raised to briny perfection. They are so good that the Willapa Bay bivalves are shipped to Chesapeake in New England.

An oyster connoisseur, David declares, "I don't eat the oysters during the summer months; then I look forward to the first oyster of the season—that's when they're perfect!"

The Shelburne Inn will celebrate its centenary in 1996. The longest continuously operating inn in Washington, it was built to serve those travellers who journeyed from Portland via the steamer *T. J. Potter* that plied the river until 1916 when it was replaced by a ferry. To this day, The Shelburne

Doug Plummer

101

John Marshall

architectural masterpiece. They bought it all, turned to each other and asked, "Now what do we do?" The answer initially was quite simple: they would restore the farmhouse to create an inn. They gutted the old house, jacked it up, poured a new foundation and rebuilt the interior as it had been, with all its nooks and crannies. In a former long ago life, Bill had been a master engraver. His sense of proportion and skill with colors show in every fastidiously decorated room. Elegant crystal doorknobs and light fixtures came from Seattle's grand old Savoy, bevelled glass and deep basins from the Empress in Victoria. All the rooms have duvets made with the wool from Turtleback sheep; handmade rugs dot the polished wooden floors. In the foyer, hanging alongside several rave reviews from *The Los Angeles Times*, is a yellowing copy of *The Seattle Times* dated 1933. It was discovered by a neighbour who had begun to remodel his home, where it was stuffed into the wall as

insulation. The huge ad and photo show muscular, youthful Buster Crabbe, Olympic champion and star of both *Tarzan* and *Flash Gordon*. He was also Susan's father.

Theirs is a serious kitchen. The silver glistens, the linen is crisply starched, the table service is English bone china. Juices are fresh, granola is home made, and each day's main course is carefully prepared and creatively composed.

They stress locally produced food: eggs cheerfully provided by a flock of Rhode Island Reds, sometimes honey from their own hives. Their 90-year-old Pippin and Northern Spy trees, which never need spraying, bear enough fruit that they can serve the farm's own apple juice.

An old stone tower stands on the summit of Mt.

Sooke Harbour House

Holland House Inn

The Beaconsfield Inn

Oceanwood Country Inn

Yellow Point Lodge

Park Royal Hotel

Durlacher Hof

April Point Lodge

Simon Desrochers

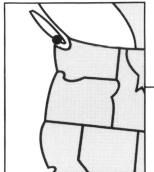

Sooke Harbour House

"The tide is out, the table is set."

Sunset cast a pink glow on the mist that curtained the Olympic Mountains. Atop a large boulder, surrounded by ocean, a bold river otter teased a bald eagle wheeling overhead. The gardens were ripe and full of color. Small seashell lights illuminated the faces of the Johnny-jump-ups. A huge mound of lavender formed a giant powder puff of purple just outside the dining room. Sensuous aromas of seafood grilling with handfuls of fresh herbs, simmering stocks and baking breads drifted from the kitchen. Candles flickered, suspended in the graceful wrought iron candelabrum. Dinner was about to be served.

I haven't eaten at all the marvelous restaurants in the Northwest, but I have eaten at virtually every Canadian inn and a good number of the finest restaurants across Canada—from the Atlantic to the Pacific. There is no other like Sooke Harbour House. Without question, the dining room in this quaintly elegant establishment is the best that we are privileged to have in Canada. Sooke Harbour House is beyond the proverbial leading edge.

Dr. Sinclair Philip has made a long-term study of unusual seafood on the wise assumption that most North Americans were used to eating only a limited variety. Although Europeans and Orientals have for centuries dined on sea urchin and gooseneck barnacles, we on this continent turned up our collective noses. For inspiration, he delved into the foodstuffs of the Northwest coastal native communities. Soon diners at Sooke Harbour House were feasting on thinly sliced abalone and purple-

Simon Desrochers

121

Bob Preston

126

and political realities of the day. Its harsh tone provides a startling tension in the refined context of the inn and its neighborhood.

The unique character of Holland House attracts a fascinating array of people. On any given day the guest list will probably include visiting lecturers from the University of Victoria, respected United Nations lawyers from Tonga who are happy to relax after the day's lectures, or Soviet lecturers rejoicing to find such elegance.

Holland House would not be possible anywhere else on earth. Lance and Robin chose the genteel, picturesque provincial capital as a place to live and work because of its climate—it has the balmiest weather in Canada—and because it is a gardener's joy.

The inn, a striking two-story building with a hip roof and expansive windows, is set in Victoria's oldest residential neighbourhood, James Bay. It is a quietly elegant area between downtown and the spectacular beachfront with its view of the distant snow-capped Olympic mountains.

Visitors have long seen Victoria, with its wide, flower-filled streets, charming alleys, engaging old buildings, and easygoing atmosphere as a walkers' dream. Holland House is walking distance from the harbor, the Parliament buildings, the Royal British Columbian Museum and the lovely 68 acre Beacon Hill park with its year-round dazzling floral display.

142

the service is discreet and the setting cannot be matched anywhere in the city. The golf-green lawns have been meticulously groomed by a fastidious Dutch gardener, Benno Gigling. Roses bloom effortlessly by the entrance. Rhododendrons and azaleas flower in profusion, nestled beside the river. Fresh herbs, particularly basil (Mario's favorite), are tucked between the rows.

Breakfasts are meant to be leisurely affairs. At least once, treat yourself to Eggs Park Royal. There have been many renditions of this classic, but chef Hans Schaub is a perfectionist and you can be guaranteed that the smoked salmon will be the best and the hollandaise will be just right. Or try the traditional British kippers with scrambled eggs.

I become somewhat nostalgic when I remember my first trip to British Columbia. The last dinner I ate before leaving "Lotus Land" was at the Park Royal, long before I knew either Mario or Angelica. I dined on huge prawns with garlic and vermouth and herb butter. I have never tasted the like. And thankfully, they are still on the menu. Why tamper with perfection? You might try the roast rack of lamb in the Dijon mustard and rosemary crust served with a spoonful of fresh mint pesto. Or there is the Fraser Valley pheasant breast in a red currant-brandy sauce.

Park Royal Hotel
540 Clyde Avenue
West Vancouver, British Columbia V7T 2J7
(604) 926–5511
FAX: (604) 926–6082
Innkeepers: Mario and Angelica Corsi

Remove from oven to wire rack. Spread with cooked apple filling.

Toss remaining apple slices with remaining sugar. Arrange in decorative pattern on top. Sprinkle with almonds. Return to oven; continue to bake for 35 minutes or until apples are tender. Place tart under broiler, three to four inches from the heat, until apples are lightly browned. Remove to wire rack.

In a small saucepan, warm the marmalade. Brush over finished tart. Cool before slicing.

MAKES SIX SERVINGS.

Kaiserschmarren

Legend has it that Emperor Franz Josef tore his pancakes into small bits, so that's how his chef served them.

> *2 c all purpose flour*
> *1 c milk*
> *¾ c unsalted butter*
> *⅛ tsp salt*
> *4 eggs, separated*
> *¼ c granulated sugar*
> *½ c raisins*
> *icing (powdered) sugar as needed*
> *stewed plums or other fruit*

In a large mixing bowl, stir together flour and milk. Melt one-fourth cup of the butter; whisk in with salt and egg yolks. In a separate bowl, beat egg whites with sugar until very stiff. Fold into batter. Melt remaining butter in 12 inch round cast-iron skillet. Pour in batter; scatter with raisins. *Preheat oven to 375°F.* Bake for 20 minutes or until puffy and golden. Tear apart with two forks. Let stand for three or four minutes before dusting with icing sugar and serving with stewed fruit.

MAKES FOUR SERVINGS.

Lemon Poppyseed Cake

When buying poppyseeds, purchase only as much as you will use in the next two or three weeks, or store larger amounts in the freezer. The oils go rancid very quickly when held at room temperature.

Cake

> *2 c all purpose flour*
> *1 Tbl baking powder*
> *1 ¼ c granulated sugar*
> *½ tsp salt*
> *¼ c poppyseeds*
> *½ c vegetable oil*
> *5 large eggs, separated*
> *¾ c milk*
> *2 tsp vanilla*
> *2 tsp lemon rind*
> *1 tsp lemon juice*
> *¼ tsp cream of tartar*

Quick Lemon Glaze

> *1 Tbl butter, softened*
> *1 c icing (powdered) sugar*
> *2 Tbl warm water*
> *2 tsp lemon rind*
> *1 tsp lemon juice*
> *additional grated lemon rind as needed*

In a large bowl, combine flour, baking powder, sugar, salt and poppyseeds. Make a well in center. Whisk together oil, egg yolks, milk, vanilla, lemon rind and lemon juice. Add to dry ingredients stirring until smooth. In a separate bowl beat egg whites with cream of tartar until stiff peaks are formed. Gently fold into batter. *Preheat oven to 325°F.* Pour into well-greased and floured bundt pan. Bake for 45 to 50 minutes or until a toothpick inserted in center comes out clean. Let cool for 15 minutes before removing from pan.

Meanwhile whisk together butter, icing sugar, water, lemon rind and juice. Drizzle warm cake with glaze and sprinkle with lemon rind.

MAKES TEN TO TWELVE SERVINGS.

April Point Lodge

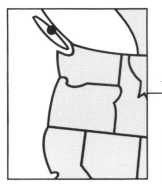

April Point Lodge has become part of my life. After travelling for a decade across Canada, searching out new inns and writing on our superb regional foods, I come back to the lodge and wonder why I ever bothered to leave. There is so much depth to the hospitality here. The Petersons have a genuine sense of history and a tremendous sense of how they fit into island life. There are four generations who are still actively involved. Phyllis Peterson, now the silver-haired matriarch, came to Quadra Island with her husband and children in 1946, before electricity and even telephone connections. Ferry service didn't link them to the mainland until 1965. April Point is first and foremost a salmon fishing lodge, a place for purists who are into the sport rather than the kill. To catch a 25 pound spring salmon on light tackle, to play it and to win is a thrill of a lifetime. You might cast all day and not have a strike, but when that streak of silver plunges through the surface to hit the bucktail, you know you have waited forever for just that moment.

The teaching component of a fishing expedition cannot be over-emphasized. Tell the Petersons what fishy skill you'd like to learn and they will assign the appropriate guide. From those who have never held a rod, to experts who have fished the oceans of the world, there is someone to add another level to your knowledge.

Meals are substantial and homemade. Breakfast begins before the first boats leave at 6:00am and continues until almost noon. Eat lunch at the lodge or order a picnic basket the evening before, throw in a beer or a chilled bottle of wine and have your guide barbecue your catch on a remote island beach.

Twice a week, Eric Peterson dons the chef's apron and fires up a huge barbecue on the broad deck beside the water. He'll pan fry you a few Cortes Island oysters to whet your appetite before grilling thick steaks, tender rosemary marinated lamb and alder smoked salmon. On other nights, the menu may vary from local spot prawns in a ginger blackberry sauce and supremely simple chilled Dungeness crab to roasted duckling and prime rib with Yorkshire pudding.

It just makes sense that sushi would become a lodge specialty. The sushi chef waits until the last moment before service to determine just which fish are perfect. There is always rich sockeye for the Tyee roll, a combination of avocado, Dungeness crab and salmon wrapped in nori (a processed seaweed), then rolled in sake-laced sticky rice and flying fish roe. Sometimes prawns are substituted for the fresh salmon to create the popular April Point roll.

Like the *entrées*, desserts change nightly. Seasonal berries are doused with cream. A fluffy chocolate cappuccino mousse cake will satisfy any addiction. And, shades of the 50s, you can order the tallest, gooiest butterscotch or chocolate sundae you've ever plunged a spoon into.

April Point Lodge

Box 1
Campbell River, British Columbia V9W 4Z9
(604) 285–2222
FAX: (604) 285–2411
Innkeepers: Phyllis, Heidi, Eric
and Warren Peterson

149

Eric's Amazing Wild Huckleberry Butter Sauce for Barbecued Salmon

Huckleberries grow everywhere on Quadra Island. Their tartness is a perfect counterpoint for the richness of barbecued salmon.

> 2 Tbl olive oil or clarified butter
> ¼ c minced shallots or green onions
> 1 c dry white wine
> 1 c fish or chicken stock
> 1 Tbl grated fresh ginger
> 1 ½ tsp freshly ground pepper
> 1 ¼ c fresh or frozen huckleberries
> 1 tsp liquid honey
> 1 Tbl apple cider vinegar
> 1 c unsalted butter, chilled and cut into small bits
> salt to taste
> 6–8 salmon fillets
> additional fresh huckleberries for garnish

In a large skillet heat olive oil or butter. *Sauté* shallots until tender but not browned, about three minutes. Increase heat to high; add wine, stock, ginger, pepper, one cup of the huckleberries, honey and vinegar. Bring to boil and cook, stirring constantly, until reduced to almost syrupy.

Remove from heat; press pulp through a strainer. Return sauce essence to skillet; bring to rapid boil. Remove from heat; whisk in butter a few bits at a time until a smooth, glossy sauce is created. Add salt to taste. Stir in remaining huckleberries. Keep warm over hot, but not boiling water.

Meanwhile, barbecue salmon, skin side down, over medium low heat until firm to touch, about six to eight minutes.

Spoon sauce onto heated plates, carefully transfer salmon into center and drizzle with a little additional sauce. Garnish with fresh huckleberries.

MAKES SIX TO EIGHT SERVINGS.

April Point Salmon Chowder

This is the best salmon chowder I have ever made. Once you master this recipe, treat it as a basic formula for other chowders. You won't be disappointed.

1 lb salmon fillet
2 Tbl butter
1 carrot, peeled and cut into matchstick sized pieces
1 stalk celery, diced
2–3 potatoes, peeled and diced
5 c fish or chicken stock
½ tsp thyme
1 bay leaf
2 Tbl tomato paste
¼ c minced parsley
1 Tbl minced capers
sour cream as needed for garnish

Remove any bones from salmon fillet. Cut into half inch cubes and set aside. In a heavy saucepan, melt butter over medium low heat. Add carrot, celery and potatoes. Cover and allow vegetables to steam in their own juices for four or five minutes or until almost tender. Add stock, thyme, bay leaf; simmer for 10 minutes. Remove bay leaf before adding salmon cubes and tomato paste. Let simmer an additional five minutes or until salmon begins to flake. Stir in parsley and minced capers. Serve hot with dollops of sour cream in the center.

MAKES FOUR SERVINGS.

Mrs. Peterson's Cinnamon Sticky Buns

The first time I visited the Lodge, the meals were so incredible that I simply couldn't manage breakfast before catching the 8:00am ferry. Eric said good-bye by handing me a large, foil-wrapped package of Mrs. P.'s cinnamon buns.

¾ c warm water
1 tsp granulated sugar
2 Tbl active dry yeast
3 eggs, well beaten
½ c granulated sugar (second amount)
½ c melted shortening
2 tsp salt
1 ¼ c warm milk
6–7 c all purpose flour
2 Tbl soft butter
⅔ c brown sugar
1–2 tsp cinnamon
⅔ c raisins
melted butter as needed
Almond Butter Icing (recipe follows)

Almond Butter Icing
¼ c softened butter
2–3 c icing (powdered) sugar
1 tsp almond extract
½ tsp vanilla extract
milk or table cream as needed

Place the warm water into a small bowl; stir in sugar and sprinkle with yeast. Set aside to rise for 10 minutes.

Whisk in beaten eggs, granulated sugar, shortening, salt and milk. Gradually beat in flour until dough is no longer sticky. Turn out onto floured board; knead three to five minutes or until dough is smooth and elastic. Return to oiled bowl, cover and let rise until doubled in bulk, about an hour and a half. Punch down; turn out onto floured board.

Divide dough in half. Roll into two 8 by 14 inch rectangles. Spread each generously with butter, brown sugar, cinnamon and raisins. Roll up lengthwise and slice into 12 pieces. Place no more than one inch apart on well-greased or parchment-lined baking sheet; cover and let rise until doubled, about 60 minutes. *Preheat oven to 350°F.* Bake for 20 to 25 minutes or until a rich golden brown. Brush with melted butter; let cool before icing.

For icing, in a large bowl, combine butter, icing sugar and almond and vanilla extract. Whisk in enough milk to make a thin frosting. Drizzle over cinnamon buns.

MAKES TWO DOZEN.

Index